M000032061

DAILY
LIFE
JOURNAL

A RESOURCE FOR MEETING
DAILY AND DEEPLY WITH GOD

DALE EVRIST & JOEL EVRIST

CORE4
SERIES

Copyright © 2019 by Dale Evrist and Joel Evrist
Cover design by Macey Fernandez and Ronda Waters
Layout design by Sarah Siegand

All rights reserved. Except as permitted by the US Copyright Act
of 1976, no part of this book may be reproduced, distributed, or
transmitted without prior written permission from the authors.
For information please contact lifereach@newsongnashville.com.

Printed in the United States of America.
ISBN: 9781710353259

Unless otherwise indicated, all scripture quotations are taken from The
New King James Version®, NKJV®, Copyright © 1979, 1980, 1982,
Thomas Nelson, Inc. Used by permission.
All rights reserved worldwide.

The "Walking Through the Word Daily Reading and Study Guide"
was adapted from the Two Year Bible (NLT)
© 2001 by Tyndale House Publishers, Inc.

TABLE OF CONTENTS

1   Introduction: A Theology of Place

5   Lesson 1: Welcome to the Secret Place

11   Lesson 2: How to Use Your Daily Life Journal in the Secret Place

17   Lesson 3: How to Walk Through the Word in the Secret Place

23   Lesson 4: How to Pray in the Secret Place

29   Lesson 5: How to Praise in the Secret Place

35   Lesson 6: How to Journal Your Journey in the Secret Place

41   Walking Through the Word Daily Reading & Study Guide

xx   Daily Journal

xx   Appendix: Scriptures for Common Prayer Needs

Introduction

A THEOLOGY
OF PLACE

INTRODUCTION:
A THEOLOGY OF PLACE

The Bible teaches that there are three main places that we are to engage in ministry unto the Lord and unto others: *The Secret Place, The Gathering Place and The Public Place*. It is important that we develop a sound *Theology of Place*, recognizing where we are to go and what we are to do to live our lives for the glory of God and the good of others, place by place, purpose by purpose and person by person.

1. THE SECRET PLACE

❏ Read Matthew 6:6

In *the Secret Place* we are to meet alone with God the Father and Jesus the Son by the life and leading of the Holy Spirit. *The Secret Place* is a place where a private, personal and intimate relationship with God can be cultivated in the Word and in prayer and praise. It is in *the Secret Place* where a private spiritual history is established, which then becomes a public spiritual history in *the Gathering Place* and *the Public Place*.

2. THE GATHERING PLACE

❏ Read Matthew 18:18-20; 1 Corinthians 14:26

In *the Gathering Place* we are to come together with the people of God, gathered in the name of Jesus, looking to minister to one another according to the truth of the Word and the person and power of the Holy Spirit. These gatherings can be as small as two or as many as thousands who agree together for the presence of Jesus to reveal and release His light and life. From *the Gathering Place* we move to *the Public Place*.

3. THE PUBLIC PLACE

❑ Read Acts 2:46-47

In *the Public Place* we release to a lost and broken world a relevant witness from a revived people—a people full of the Word and the Spirit, received in *the Secret Place* and *the Gathering Place*. It is in this place where a *Theology of Place* finds its point of missional completion as neighbors, nations and generations are reached with the good news of Jesus Christ's love and power, person by person, need by need.

In establishing a sound *Theology of Place*, this resource will help you to focus on *the Secret Place*, which is the first place that prepares you to engage *the Gathering Place* and *the Public Place*. For it is in *the Secret Place* that we meet with God daily and deeply, which becomes the foundation and the spiritual force that enables us to be fully effective in *the Gathering Place* and *the Public Place*.

The *Daily Life Journal* is a resource that will guide you in engaging and encountering God in prayer and praise and in walking and working through the Word. Additionally, it will instruct you on how to journal your journey with God the Father, Jesus the Son and the Holy Spirit in living each day with a sense of divine purpose and dynamic direction.

DAILY LIFE JOURNAL

Notes

...IT IS IN THE SECRET PLACE THAT WE MEET WITH GOD DAILY AND DEEPLY...

Lesson 1

WELCOME TO THE SECRET PLACE

1

WELCOME TO THE SECRET PLACE

DISCOVERING THE PURPOSE AND PRIVILEGE OF THE SECRET PLACE

❑ Read Psalm 27:4-5; Psalm 91:1-2; Matthew 6:5-6

All of us have been created on purpose for purpose – to know God intimately forever. In the Old Testament, every ritual, commandment and celebration declared the knowledge of God's character and drew people into a pursuit of knowing God more deeply. In the New Testament, the perfect life, atoning death and victorious resurrection of Jesus Christ provided a new and living way to God, enabling people to know Him fully and completely. One glorious day in the future when the Lord's Great Commission is fulfilled, Jesus will return, and we will see Him and know Him perfectly and personally forever. Until that day, He has given us the magnificent privilege of growing in knowing Him through *the Secret Place.*

> All of us have been created on purpose for purpose – to know God intimately forever.

UNDERSTANDING THE SECRET PLACE

In Jesus' day, it was common for people to pray only

Notes

when in public. Also, people would most often only read and recite Scripture when they were in the synagogue (the local gathering place for Jews to meet for corporate worship and teaching on the Sabbath day). This was mostly due to the religious leaders of the day, who modeled public displays of piety to be seen by others and affirmed accordingly. When Jesus came to earth, He lived in a religious culture where people often sought to draw attention to their apparent devotion to God.

Into this religious culture, Jesus came calling people to a private devoted worship that would become a public dynamic witness. He called all people to first prayerfully seek the Heavenly Father in *the Secret Place*. (❏ Read Matthew 6:6.) *The Secret Place* literally means "the secret" in the original language. It means a place of solitude or a place where no one else is around. *The Secret Place* was to be a private place where Jesus called people to meet daily and deeply with God the Father. Jesus was calling and commanding all people back to the starting place of all true devotion to God, and on to a greater place and a deeper place of intimacy with God through Him.

Just as Jesus called people in the past to *the Secret Place*, so He calls you and me to this place as well. *The Secret Place* is a daily place of meeting with God, rather than a place we visit occasionally. It is both a consistent action of withdrawing to be with

This special and sacred place is where we listen, study and meditate on the Scriptures, pray, praise and journal.

God in private and a consistent attitude of waiting on Him until we hear from Him and receive what He knows we need. This special and sacred place is where we listen, study and meditate on the Scriptures, pray, praise and journal. (❏ Read Psalm 5:1-3.)

FINDING YOUR SECRET PLACE

In finding your *Secret Place*, you are first following Jesus in the way He found His. As with any of Christ's commands, He is our forerunner. In other words, He never commands us to do what He has not already done. He consistently found a private and personal place to seek the face of God for intimate fellowship and abundant revelation. He calls us to do the same. So, your *Secret Place* is really any place you can be alone. Its location can look different for all of us. The most important key to finding your *Secret Place* is to pray and ask God when and where He wants you to meet with Him each day. We want to look for a place where we can speak freely with God, pray and praise freely, kneel and bow freely, sing freely and receive from Him without distraction. While finding the where and when of your *Secret Place* may change from season to season, there is always a private and personal place where God beckons you to come and meet with Him daily and deeply. (❏ Read Mark 1:35.)

Notes

Notes

...THERE IS ALWAYS A PRIVATE AND PERSONAL PLACE WHERE GOD BECKONS YOU TO COME AND MEET WITH HIM DAILY & DEEPLY.

Lesson 2

HOW TO USE YOUR DAILY LIFE JOURNAL IN THE SECRET PLACE

2

HOW TO USE YOUR DAILY LIFE JOURNAL IN THE SECRET PLACE

Encountering the Father, Son and Holy Spirit in *the Secret Place* every day is not merely a religious ritual or rigorous routine. *The Secret Place* is a relational reality. Every word in the Word is sacred and teeming with divine life. The Holy Spirit is ready to lead you to love, look, listen, learn and live. Your *Daily Life Journal* will help you encounter and remain in the presence of God by anchoring you in the following spiritual disciplines.

LOVE

❏ Read Mark 12:29-31; John 14:21

The Bible says the Father sent His only Son to make us His sons and daughters because He loves us. Our pursuit of God in *the Secret Place* must be motivated by the same divine love. Begin each time in *the Secret Place* by asking Jesus to fill you freshly with His Holy Spirit and with His divine love. With this divine love, love the Scriptures as your inspired guide through every situation of life. With this love, love the privileged position given to you, making you able to intimately come before the throne of grace every day in prayer for yourself, your family, your friends and those in the world.

LOOK

❑ Read Psalm 63:1-2; Hebrews 12:1-2

The aim of *the Secret Place* is God's Word, will and ways. Look to God as the focus of your prayers and praise. Look into the Word of God with an eye toward investigation, interpretation, meditation, memorization and application. Look intently for the Holy Spirit's revelation in God's Word. The will of the Father, Son and Holy Spirit should be your exclusive focus in *the Secret Place*. Your mind will be tempted with distractions. When your mind begins to wander, fix your eyes on the leading of the Holy Spirit.

LISTEN

❑ Read John 16:12-15; Colossians 1:9

... keep your ear to the Holy Spirit's voice while studying the Word, praying, praising and journaling.

Perhaps the simplest and yet most difficult discipline in *the Secret Place*, listening is essential to hearing from God. Like a student intently listens to a tutor, keep your ear to the Holy Spirit's voice while studying the Word, praying, praising and journaling. You have no idea how much God wants to speak to you until you quiet and calm yourself to wait, listen and heed what you hear.

Notes

LEARN

❑ Read Psalm 119:1; 2 Timothy 2:15

Using a trusted study Bible in a reliable and understandable translation and the Walking Through The Word Daily Reading an Study Guide in your *Daily Life Journal*, ask the Holy Spirit to teach you new things every day from His Word. Using the journal pages, write down points of investigation (what the text says), interpretation (what the text means), and application (how you will respond and obey). As the Holy Spirit highlights specific Scripture verses, write them down to mediate on and memorize. Learn by listening to the *Walking Through the Word* podcast with Pastor Dale Evrist.[1] This book by book audio commentary will teach you exciting new things about the scriptures you're reading each day and how to lovingly obey God's Word.

LIVE

❑ Read Matthew 7:24-25; James 1:22-25

Live out what you have received in *the Secret Place* by taking your *Daily Life Journal* with you wherever you go as a reference and reminder of what you heard and wrote down. Live out what you have received in *the Secret Place* by looking for opportunities to share it with others in *the Gathering Place* and *the Public Place*. As you looked to and listened to the Holy Spirit in *the Secret Place*, continue letting the Holy Spirit lead you into living out in public what you received in private.

[1] To access, search in your mobile app for "Walking Through the Word Podcast, Dale Evrist."

Notes

Notes

...CONTINUE LETTING THE HOLY SPIRIT LEAD YOU INTO LIVING OUT IN PUBLIC WHAT YOU RECEIVED IN PRIVATE.

Lesson 3

HOW TO WALK THROUGH THE WORD IN THE SECRET PLACE

3

HOW TO WALK THROUGH THE WORD IN THE SECRET PLACE

❏ Read 2 Timothy 3:16-17

Walking through the Word has to do with reading the Bible through from Genesis to Revelation for the purpose of becoming more and more familiar with the full scope of God's divine revelation to mankind through the Scriptures. Regardless of how many times you read through God's Word, there are always new and fresh revelations to be discovered and applied. God's Word is an inexhaustible source of daily wisdom and spiritual understanding.

> ... there are always new and fresh revelations to be discovered and applied.

As you daily walk through the Word utilizing the Walking Through The Word Daily Reading and Study Guide included in this resource, the following guidelines will help you better understand what each passage of scripture is saying, what it means, how it transforms you and how to apply it.

INVESTIGATION

Investigation teaches you to see exactly what the passage says. It is the basis for accurate interpretation and correct application. Investigation answers the question, "What does the passage say?" Thorough investigation includes paying attention to the words that are used, watching for points of emphasis and repetition.

INTERPRETATION

While investigation leads to an accurate understanding of what the Word of God says, interpretation goes a step further and helps you understand what it means in the context in which it was written as well as the definitions of the words being used. This can be more thoroughly accomplished through the use of trusted study Bibles and Bible commentaries.

MEDITATION

As you discover what the Word says in investigation and what the Word means in interpretation, you move into how the Word transforms your intellect, emotion and will through meditation. Meditation is about allowing the Holy Spirit to deeply embed truth unto transformation as you think, listen and speak repeatedly the things that the Spirit is underscoring and emphasizing. Memorization should flow out of meditation as you allow God's Word to shape and change your life.

APPLICATION

Having engaged in investigation, interpretation and meditation, the next step is application. Once you understand what the Word of God says and means and have allowed the Holy Spirit to deeply embed it in your understanding, application – putting these things into daily practice – becomes the goal of investigation, interpretation and meditation.

Notes

Notes

WALKING THROUGH THE WORD PODCAST[1]

A resource that can help you in daily walking through the Word is Pastor Dale Evrist's devotional commentary on the scriptures read each day in the Walking Through The Word Daily Reading and Study Guide. This podcast resource is offered as an additional way to help you apply the truths that are contained in the Word of God. The *Walking Through the Word* podcast will help you to both more clearly understand and more personally and practically apply the daily passages that you are reading.

[1]To access, search in your mobile app for "Walking Through the Word Podcast, Dale Evrist."

Notes

Notes

GOD'S WORD IS AN INEXHAUSTIBLE SOURCE OF DAILY WISDOM & SPIRITUAL UNDER-STANDING.

Lesson 4

HOW TO PRAY IN THE SECRET PLACE

4

HOW TO PRAY IN THE SECRET PLACE

❏ Read Luke 11:1-4

Praying the Word and praying according to the Word are the soundest and surest ways to ensure that our praying is according to the will and ways of God. Praying in this manner gives our praying both divine accuracy and authority. It anchors our minds in truth and fills our hearts with peace and assurance that our praying will be acted on and answered.

Jesus' disciples asked Him to teach them how to pray and what to pray. Jesus' response was to give them both a pattern for prayer as well as powerful words to use in their praying. This pattern for prayer is offered as a path and a guide to help you in daily and dynamically praying in *the Secret Place.* The following will lead you into a life of praying the way Jesus taught.

> ... daily and dynamically praying in *the Secret Place.*

❏ Read Matthew 6:9-13

"OUR FATHER IN HEAVEN" | Affirm your identity as a child of God.

"HALLOWED BE YOUR NAME" | *Hallowed* means held in awe or revered. Praise and thank God for who He is, what He has done and what He will do. As the Holy Spirit leads, include in your prayer the names of God:

THE NAMES OF GOD:

- **El Elyon | "God Most High"**
  (❏ Read Genesis 14:18)

- **El Roi | "God Who Sees"**
  (❏ Read Genesis 16:13)

- **El Shaddai | "God Almighty"**
  (❏ Read Genesis 17:1)

- **Yahweh Jireh | "The Lord Will Provide"**
  (❏ Read Genesis 22:14)

- **Yahweh Rophe | "The Lord Who Heals"**
  (❏ Read Exodus 15:26)

- **Yahweh Nissi | "The Lord My Banner"**
  (❏ Read Exodus 17:15)

- **Yahweh M'Kaddesh | "The Lord Who Sanctifies You"** (❏ Read Exodus 31:13)

- **Yahweh Shalom | "The Lord Is Peace"**
  (❏ Read Judges 6:24)

- **Yahweh Rohi | "The Lord My Shepherd"**
  (❏ Read Psalm 23:1)

- **Yahweh Tsidkenu | "The Lord Our Righteousness"** (❏ Read Jeremiah 23:6)

- **Yahweh Sabaoth | "The Lord of Hosts"**
  (❏ Read 1 Samuel 1:3)

- **Yahweh Shammah | "The Lord Is There"**
  (❏ Read Ezekiel 48:35)

Notes

Notes

"YOUR KINGDOM COME. YOUR WILL BE DONE ON EARTH AS IT IS IN HEAVEN" | Pray for God's purposes and plans personally, locally, nationally and globally.

"GIVE US THIS DAY OUR DAILY BREAD" | You never know how much God will get to you if He knows He can get it through you (to others). God promises to meet our needs, but we are to show our dependency on Him and ask for what we need to receive from Him for others. Pray dependently, consistently, specifically and expectantly for your and others' physical, emotional and spiritual needs.

"FORGIVE US OUR DEBTS, AS WE FORGIVE OUR DEBTORS" | Ask the Holy Spirit to show you where you need to:

- Receive God's forgiveness for your sins through repentance, confession and cleansing. (❏ Read 1 John 1:9.)

- Release God's forgiveness to others who have sinned against you and cancel their debt. (❏ Read Mark 11:25-26.)

"DO NOT LEAD US (ALLOW US TO BE LED) INTO TEMPTATION, BUT DELIVER US FROM THE EVIL ONE" | Take particular areas of temptation before the Lord, surrendering to God's strength and protection. Take authority over the enemy, committing both to resist his attacks and defeat his strategies trusting that the way of escape and the path to victory is ours in Christ Jesus.

"YOURS IS THE KINGDOM AND THE POWER AND THE GLORY FOREVER" |

- **The Kingdom:** Rest in the knowledge that Christ's rule and dominion are working through and around us.

- **The Power:** Rely on God's dynamic power provided by the Holy Spirit in everything at all times.

- **The Glory:** Reflect and represent God's excellence and splendor to the world.

Notes

REFLECT
AND
REPRESENT
GOD'S
EXCELLENCE AND
SPLENDOR
IN THE
WORLD.

HOW TO PRAISE IN THE SECRET PLACE

5

HOW TO PRAISE IN THE SECRET PLACE

The Secret Place isn't necessarily a quiet place. It is a safe place. It is a private place. It is a place of calm and comfort. It may be quiet at times, but it's also to be a place of praise—declared and described. This was true of King David and all the psalmists and should be true of us as well. We must follow the examples of these men and countless others throughout the Scriptures and church history who used *the Secret Place* for the release of God's praise.

David declared that *the Secret Place* would be a place of both prayer and praise. (❑ Read Psalm 27.) He wrote that he would cry out to God in passionate and faith-filled prayer. He also wrote that he would offer songs of praise as sacrifices of joyous shouts concerning God's great goodness. Those who served most closely with King David would have undoubtedly heard his voice lifted in praise each and every day. He began with praise in the morning and ended with praise at the end of the day. He was never trying to guard his dignity but always endeavoring to give the glory to the God he loved and served.

PRAISE IN THE SECRET PLACE SHOULD BE EARLY

Praise in *the Secret Place* should begin in the morning. (❑ Read Psalm 5:1-3; 63:1-6.) We should begin each day by declaring who God is and describing what He has done. David declared that God was the God of every day and that He would be God throughout the day. When you read the psalms written by David, it is obvious that he believed that every day was to be welcomed with worship beginning with blessing the Lord as his Savior and source.

And throughout the Scriptures, people are seen as beginning the day by seeking God and committing their days and their lives to their God. (❑ Read Mark 1:35.) Beginning the day with praise sets the course for honoring God for everything and in everything.

> We should begin each day by declaring who God is and describing what He has done.

PRAISE IN THE SECRET PLACE SHOULD BE EXPRESSIVE

King David declared that praise should be spoken from grateful lips, lifted with holy hands and demonstrated with every possible part of human expression. The term *bless* means to ascribe the blessings in life to God as their source. Lifting glad and grateful praise to the blessed God is a righteous expression of truth and love. Our God is worthy and is worthy to be praised every day and in every way.

PRAISE IN THE SECRET PLACE SHOULD BE EXTENSIVE

The praise of God should be from morning until night. David said that he would book-end his days with praise. Praise would begin at the rising of the sun and end at the setting of the sun. He did not see praise as an isolated event but as an integrated lifestyle. David saw *the Secret Place* as a place to begin the day and to end the day—leading to praise throughout the day. David extended praise from *the Secret Place* to *the Gathering Place* to *the Public Place*.

PRAISE IN THE SECRET PLACE SHOULD BE EXTRAVAGANT

We are called to approach God with lavish thanksgiving and praise. (❑ Read Psalm 100:1-5.) We are to enter every encounter with God with praise poured out in abundant love and gratitude generously released. When we begin our day in *the Secret Place* with praise that is fitting and freely released for our worthy God and King Jesus, we are better able to represent Him well throughout the rest of the day.

The ministry of prayer and praise is consistent with our calling as priests and servants of the Most High God. (❑ Read 1 Peter 2:4-5.) Let's lift up strong and clear praise to God at the start of each day. Then, let's lift Him up throughout the day until the end of the day. From the rising of the sun until it sets, let God be praised.

> We are called to approach God with lavish thanksgiving and praise.

Notes

Notes

FROM THE
RISING
OF THE
SUN UNTIL
IT SETS,
LET
GOD BE
PRAISED.

Lesson 6

HOW TO JOURNAL YOUR JOURNEY IN THE SECRET PLACE

6

HOW TO JOURNAL YOUR JOURNEY IN THE SECRET PLACE

❑ Read Habakkuk 2:1-4

The prophet Habakkuk was a man in need of prophetic insights, answers, vision and strategies. He posed a number of questions to God concerning himself, his people and the world around him. He was concerned about some things and confused about some others, but he was committed to God and following whatever His Word, will and ways would reveal to him. He wisely realized that his view of things was limited, and he was open to embrace whatever correction unto greater clarity that God would speak to Him. God not only spoke to him in a way that he could understand, He instructed him to record in writing what He was being shown, not only for his sake but for the sake of others as well. It was in Habakkuk's committing to *journal his journey* with God that he and others were able to receive clear vision and move in a clear direction unto its fulfillment.

The Sons of Korah declared that they would both speak and write concerning the beauty, majesty and glory of the king and his bride, which prophetically spoke of the ultimate King, the Lord Jesus, and His bride, the Church. (❑ Read Psalm 45:1-17.) We can use their words today to praise and extol the greatness of King Jesus and the blessings of His cherished and chosen people because of their faithfulness to *journal their journey,* speaking

48

forth and writing down the richness of the revelation they received.

In the Gospel of Luke and the book of Acts, Luke writes an orderly and detailed account of the life and ministry of Jesus and the work of the Holy Spirit in and through the lives of His followers. (❏ Read Luke 1:1-4; Acts 1:1-3.) Because he wrote and journaled well, we have a handbook and a guidebook on how to follow Jesus and live by the person and power of the Holy Spirit.

JOURNALING YOUR JOURNEY WITH JESUS

While journaling your journey with Jesus would not be considered Scripture, it is still to be rooted in the Scriptures and led by the Holy Spirit. Creating a written record of the things God reveals to you in *the Secret Place* serves as a way to help you track your prophetic progress in growing in grace and revelational knowledge of God and His plans, purposes and promises for you. The journal pages in this *Daily Life Journal* will help you to that end. Use the following as a guide as you *journal your journey in the Secret Place:*

... track your prophetic progress in growing in grace and revelational knowledge of God and His plans, purposes and promises for you.

Notes

JOURNAL YOUR JOURNEY DAILY

Every day represents a fresh and new opportunity to record the revelations you are receiving by the Word and the Spirit, and the ways in which your relationship with the Father, Son and Holy Spirit is growing. Try not to miss a day of recording unto remembering the work of God in your life. (☐ Read Lamentations 3:22-24.)

JOURNAL YOUR JOURNEY DEEPLY

Be as detailed as you can in journaling the depth of what God is saying and doing each day. Commit yourself to *going deep and growing strong* in the grace and knowledge of your Lord and Savior Jesus Christ. (☐ Read 2 Peter 3:18.)

JOURNAL YOUR JOURNEY DYNAMICALLY

Your journaling is not to be a dull exercise but rather a dynamic expression of your intimacy with God. Let your journaling be words of life and love that reflect the genuine work of God's Spirit in and through you. (☐ Read 2 Corinthians 3:17-18.)

JOURNAL YOUR JOURNEY DEVOTEDLY

God has not called you to be *devoted to discipline,* but to be *disciplined to devotion.* For it is out of our devotion to God the Father, God the Son and God the Holy Spirit that we become disciplined and dynamic followers of Jesus. Let your journaling flow out of a heart dedicated and devoted to Him. (☐ Read Philippians 3:7-11.)

Notes

Notes

COMMIT
YOURSELF
TO GOING
DEEP AND
GROWING STRONG
IN THE GRACE &
KNOWLEDGE
OF YOUR
LORD &
SAVIOR
JESUS
CHRIST.

Two-Year

WALKING THROUGH THE WORD DAILY READING & STUDY GUIDE

JANUARY

YEAR ONE

Day	OT	NT	Psalms	Proverbs
☐ 1	Genesis 1:1-2:3	Matthew 1:1-17	1:1-5	1:1-6
☐ 2	Genesis 2:4-25	Matthew 1:18-25	1:6	1:7-9
☐ 3	Genesis 3:1-24	Matthew 2:1-12	2:1-6	1:10-19
☐ 4	Genesis 4:1-26	Matthew 2:13-23	2:7-12	1:20-23
☐ 5	Genesis 5:1-32	Matthew 3:1-6	3:1-5	1:24-28
☐ 6	Genesis 6:1-22	Matthew 3:7-17	3:6-8	1:29-33
☐ 7	Genesis 7:1-24	Matthew 4:1-11	4:1-3	2:1-5
☐ 8	Genesis 8:1-9:19	Matthew 4:12-22	4:4-8	2:6-15
☐ 9	Genesis 9:20-10:32	Matthew 4:23-25	5:1-6	2:16-22
☐ 10	Genesis 11:1-26	Matthew 5:1-12	5:7-12	3:1-6
☐ 11	Genesis 11:27-13:4	Matthew 5:13-26	6:1-5	3:7-8
☐ 12	Genesis 13:5-14:16	Matthew 5:27-37	6:6-10	3:9-10
☐ 13	Genesis 14:17-15:21	Matthew 5:38-48	7:1-9	3:11-12
☐ 14	Genesis 16:1-17:14	Matthew 6:1-13	7:10-17	3:13-15
☐ 15	Genesis 17:15-18:15	Matthew 6:14-24	8:1	3:16-18
☐ 16	Genesis 18:16-19:26	Matthew 6:25-7:6	8:2-9	3:19-20
☐ 17	Genesis 19:27-38	Matthew 7:7-14	9:1-8	3:21-26
☐ 18	Genesis 20:1-21:21	Matthew 7:15-23	9:9-12	3:27-32
☐ 19	Genesis 21:22-22:24	Matthew 7:24-29	9:13-18	3:33-35
☐ 20	Genesis 23:1-20	Matthew 8:1-4	9:19-20	4:1-6
☐ 21	Genesis 24:1-51	Matthew 8:5-17	10:1-6	4:7-10
☐ 22	Genesis 24:52-25:28	Matthew 8:18-27	10:7-15	4:11-13
☐ 23	Genesis 25:29-26:16	Matthew 8:28-34	10:16	4:14-19
☐ 24	Genesis 26:17-35	Matthew 9:1-8	10:17-18	4:20-27
☐ 25	Genesis 27:1-45	Matthew 9:9-17	11:1-6	5:1-6
☐ 26	Genesis 27:46-28:22	Matthew 9:18-26	11:7	5:7-14
☐ 27	Genesis 29:1-35	Matthew 9:27-38	12:1-5	5:15-21
☐ 28	Genesis 30:1-24	Matthew 10:1-4	12:6-8	5:22-23
☐ 29	Genesis 30:25-31:16	Matthew 10:5-23	13:1-4	6:1-5
☐ 30	Genesis 31:17-55	Matthew 10:24-39	13:5-6	6:6-11
☐ 31	Genesis 32:1-12	Matthew 10:40-11:6	14:1-6	6:12-15

FEBRUARY

YEAR ONE

Day	OT	NT	Psalms	Proverbs
1	Genesis 32:13-33:20	Matthew 11:7-19	14:7	6:16-19
2	Genesis 34:1-31	Matthew 11:20-30	15:1-5	6:20-26
3	Genesis 35:1-36:8	Matthew 12:1-8	16:1-4	6:27-35
4	Genesis 36:9-43	Matthew 12:9-21	16:5-8	7:1-5
5	Genesis 37:1-36	Matthew 12:22-32	16:9-11	7:6-23
6	Genesis 38:1-30	Matthew 12:33-45	17:1-5	7:24-27
7	Genesis 39:1-23	Matthew 12:46-13:9	17:6-15	8:1-11
8	Genesis 40:1-41:16	Matthew 13:10-23	18:1-3	8:12-13
9	Genesis 41:17-52	Matthew 13:24-33	18:4-15	8:14-26
10	Genesis 41:53-42:17	Matthew 13:34-46	18:16-24	8:27-32
11	Genesis 42:18-38	Matthew 13:47-58	18:25-36	8:33-36
12	Genesis 43:1-34	Matthew 14:1-12	18:37-45	9:1-6
13	Genesis 44:1-45:15	Matthew 14:13-21	18:46-50	9:7-8
14	Genesis 45:16-46:7	Matthew 14:22-36	19:1-6	9:9-10
15	Genesis 46:8-47:12	Matthew 15:1-14	19:7-14	9:11-12
16	Genesis 47:13-31	Matthew 15:15-28	20:1-6	9:13-18
17	Genesis 48:1-22	Matthew 15:29-39	20:7-9	10:1-2
18	Genesis 49:1-33	Matthew 16:1-12	21:1-7	10:3-4
19	Genesis 50:1-26	Matthew 16:13-20	21:8-13	10:5
20	Exodus 1:1-2:10	Matthew 16:21-17:9	22:1-18	10:6-7
21	Exodus 2:11-22	Matthew 17:10-21	22:19-24	10:8-9
22	Exodus 2:23-3:22	Matthew 17:22-27	22:25-26	10:10
23	Exodus 4:1-26	Matthew 18:1-14	22:27-31	10:11-12
24	Exodus 4:27-5:21	Matthew 18:15-22	23:1-6	10:13-14
25	Exodus 5:22-6:30	Matthew 18:23-35	24:1-2	10:15-16
26	Exodus 7:1-25	Matthew 19:1-12	24:3-6	10:17
27	Exodus 8:1-32	Matthew 19:13-25	24:7-10	10:18
28*	Exodus 9:1-35	Matthew 19:26-30	25:1-7	10:19

Note: When Leap Year occurs, divide the February 28 reading between February 28 and February 29.

MARCH

YEAR ONE

Day	OT	NT	Psalms	Proverbs
☐ 1	Exodus 10:1-29	Matthew 20:1-16	25:8-15	10:20-21
☐ 2	Exodus 11:1-12:13	Matthew 20:17-28	25:16-22	10:22
☐ 3	Exodus 12:14-39	Matthew 20:29-21:11	26:1-8	10:23
☐ 4	Exodus 12:40-13:16	Matthew 21:12-22	26:9-12	10:24-25
☐ 5	Exodus 13:17-14:31	Matthew 21:23-32	27:1	10:26
☐ 6	Exodus 15:1-18	Matthew 21:33-46	27:2-3	10:27-28
☐ 7	Exodus 15:19-16:18	Matthew 22:1-22	27:4-6	10:29-30
☐ 8	Exodus 16:19-17:16	Matthew 22:23-33	27:7-10	10:31-32
☐ 9	Exodus 18:1-12	Matthew 22:34-46	27:11-14	11:1-3
☐ 10	Exodus 18:13-19:15	Matthew 23:1-12	28:1-5	11:4
☐ 11	Exodus 19:16-20:26	Matthew 23:13-26	28:6-9	11:5-6
☐ 12	Exodus 21:1-21	Matthew 23:27-39	29:1-2	11:7
☐ 13	Exodus 21:22-22:13	Matthew 24:1-14	29:3-11	11:8
☐ 14	Exodus 22:14-23:13	Matthew 24:15-28	30:1-3	11:9-11
☐ 15	Exodus 23:14-24:2	Matthew 24:29-36	30:4-12	11:12-13
☐ 16	Exodus 24:3-25:30	Matthew 24:37-51	31:1-2	11:14
☐ 17	Exodus 25:31-26:29	Matthew 25:1-13	31:3-8	11:15
☐ 18	Exodus 26:30-27:21	Matthew 25:14-30	31:9-18	11:16-17
☐ 19	Exodus 28:1-14	Matthew 25:31-46	31:19-20	11:18-19
☐ 20	Exodus 28:15-43	Matthew 26:1-13	31:21-22	11:20-21
☐ 21	Exodus 29:1-28	Matthew 26:14-25	31:23-24	11:22
☐ 22	Exodus 29:29-30:10	Matthew 26:26-46	32:1-7	11:23
☐ 23	Exodus 30:11-38	Matthew 26:47-56	32:8-11	11:24-26
☐ 24	Exodus 31:1-18	Matthew 26:57-68	33:1-5	11:27
☐ 25	Exodus 32:1-30	Matthew 26:69-75	33:6-11	11:28
☐ 26	Exodus 32:31-33:23	Matthew 27:1-14	33:12-19	11:29-31
☐ 27	Exodus 34:1-14	Matthew 27:15-26	33:20-22	12:1
☐ 28	Exodus 34:15-35:9	Matthew 27:27-31	34:1-3	12:2-3
☐ 29	Exodus 35:10-36:7	Matthew 27:32-53	34:4-10	12:4
☐ 30	Exodus 36:8-38	Matthew 27:54-66	34:11-14	12:5-7
☐ 31	Exodus 37:1-38:8	Matthew 28:1-10	34:15-22	12:8-9

APRIL

YEAR ONE

Day	OT	NT	Psalms	Proverbs
1	Exodus 38:9-31	Matthew 28:11-20	35:1-9	12:10
2	Exodus 39:1-43	Mark 1:1-15	35:10-18	12:11
3	Exodus 40:1-38	Mark 1:16-28	35:19-28	12:12-14
4	Leviticus 1:1-17	Mark 1:29-45	36:1-5	12:15-17
5	Leviticus 2:1-3:17	Mark 2:1-12	36:6-9	12:18
6	Leviticus 4:1-26	Mark 2:13-22	36:10-12	12:19-20
7	Leviticus 4:27-5:19	Mark 2:23-3:6	37:1-6	12:21-23
8	Leviticus 6:1-23	Mark 3:7-19	37:7-11	12:24
9	Leviticus 6:24-7:27	Mark 3:20-30	37:12-20	12:25
10	Leviticus 7:28-8:17	Mark 3:31-4:9	37:21-29	12:26
11	Leviticus 8:18-9:6	Mark 4:10-25	37:30-33	12:27-28
12	Leviticus 9:7-24	Mark 4:26-41	37:34-40	13:1
13	Leviticus 10:1-20	Mark 5:1-20	38:1-18	13:2-3
14	Leviticus 11:1-47	Mark 5:21-34	38:19-22	13:4
15	Leviticus 12:1-8	Mark 5:35-43	39:1-5	13:5-6
16	Leviticus 13:1-23	Mark 6:1-15	39:6-13	13:7-8
17	Leviticus 13:24-59	Mark 6:16-29	40:1-3	13:9-10
18	Leviticus 14:1-32	Mark 6:30-44	40:4-10	13:11
19	Leviticus 14:33-57	Mark 6:45-56	40:11-13	13:12-14
20	Leviticus 15:1-33	Mark 7:1-8	40:14-17	13:15-16
21	Leviticus 16:1-28	Mark 7:9-23	41:1-3	13:17-19
22	Leviticus 16:29-17:16	Mark 7:24-8:10	41:4-13	13:20-23
23	Leviticus 18:1-30	Mark 8:11-26	42:1-8	13:24-25
24	Leviticus 19:1-34	Mark 8:27-38	42:9-11	14:1-2
25	Leviticus 19:35-20:21	Mark 9:1-13	43:1-4	14:3-4
26	Leviticus 20:22-21:24	Mark 9:14-29	43:5	14:5-6
27	Leviticus 22:1-16	Mark 9:30-37	44:1-3	14:7-8
28	Leviticus 22:17-23:21	Mark 9:38-50	44:4-8	14:9-10
29	Leviticus 23:22-44	Mark 10:1-12	44:9-22	14:11-12
30	Leviticus 24:1-25:13	Mark 10:13-16	44:23-26	14:13-14

MAY

YEAR ONE

Day	OT	NT	Psalms	Proverbs
1	Leviticus 25:14-46	Mark 10:17-31	45:1-6	14:15-16
2	Leviticus 25:47-26:13	Mark 10:32-45	45:7-17	14:17-19
3	Leviticus 26:14-46	Mark 10:46-52	46:1-7	14:20-21
4	Leviticus 27:1-34	Mark 11:1-11	46:8-11	14:22-24
5	Numbers 1:1-54	Mark 11:12-26	47:1-7	14:25
6	Numbers 2:1-3:10	Mark 11:27-33	47:8-9	14:26-27
7	Numbers 3:11-51	Mark 12:1-17	48:1-8	14:28-29
8	Numbers 4:1-49	Mark 12:18-34	48:9-14	14:30-31
9	Numbers 5:1-31	Mark 12:35-37	49:1-9	14:32-33
10	Numbers 6:1-7:9	Mark 12:38-44	49:10-20	14:34-35
11	Numbers 7:10-89	Mark 13:1-13	50:1-6	15:1-3
12	Numbers 8:1-9:3	Mark 13:14-27	50:7-23	15:4
13	Numbers 9:4-23	Mark 13:28-37	51:1-9	15:5-7
14	Numbers 10:1-36	Mark 14:1-11	51:10-19	15:8-10
15	Numbers 11:1-23	Mark 14:12-21	52:1-7	15:11
16	Numbers 11:24-12:16	Mark 14:22-31	52:8-9	15:12-14
17	Numbers 13:1-33	Mark 14:32-52	53:1-5	15:15-17
18	Numbers 14:1-25	Mark 14:53-65	53:6	15:18-19
19	Numbers 14:26-15:16	Mark 14:66-72	54:1-4	15:20-21
20	Numbers 15:17-41	Mark 15:1-24	54:5-7	15:22-23
21	Numbers 16:1-40	Mark 15:25-32	55:1-11	15:24-26
22	Numbers 16:41-18:7	Mark 15:33-47	55:12-23	15:27-28
23	Numbers 18:8-32	Mark 16:1-8	56:1-9	15:29-30
24	Numbers 19:1-22	Mark 16:9-20	56:10-13	15:31-32
25	Numbers 20:1-29	Luke 1:1-7	57:1-3	15:33
26	Numbers 21:1-30	Luke 1:8-25	57:4-11	16:1-3
27	Numbers 21:31-22:20	Luke 1:26-38	58:1-9	16:4-5
28	Numbers 22:21-41	Luke 1:39-56	58:10-11	16:6-7
29	Numbers 23:1-30	Luke 1:57-66	59:1-13	16:8-9
30	Numbers 24:1-25	Luke 1:67-80	59:14-17	16:10-11
31	Numbers 25:1-18	Luke 2:1-20	60:1-5	16:12-13

JUNE

YEAR ONE

Day	OT	NT	Psalms	Proverbs
☐ 1	Numbers 26:1-37	Luke 2:21-35	60:6-12	16:14-15
☐ 2	Numbers 26:38-51	Luke 2:36-40	61:1-3	16:16-17
☐ 3	Numbers 26:52-27:11	Luke 2:41-52	61:4-8	16:18
☐ 4	Numbers 27:12-28:15	Luke 3:1-14	62:1-8	16:19-20
☐ 5	Numbers 28:16-29:11	Luke 3:15-22	62:9-12	16:21-23
☐ 6	Numbers 29:12-40	Luke 3:23-28	63:1-5	16:24
☐ 7	Numbers 30:1-31:24	Luke 3:29-4:13	63:6-11	16:25
☐ 8	Numbers 31:25-54	Luke 4:14-30	64:1-9	16:26-27
☐ 9	Numbers 32:1-42	Luke 4:31-44	64:10	16:28-30
☐ 10	Numbers 33:1-39	Luke 5:1-11	65:1-4	16:31-33
☐ 11	Numbers 33:40-34:29	Luke 5:12-16	65:5-13	17:1
☐ 12	Numbers 35:1-34	Luke 5:17-28	66:1-7	17:2-3
☐ 13	Numbers 36:1-13	Luke 5:29-39	66:8-20	17:4-5
☐ 14	Deuteronomy 1:1-46	Luke 6:1-11	67:1-3	17:6
☐ 15	Deuteronomy 2:1-37	Luke 6:12-19	67:4-7	17:7-8
☐ 16	Deuteronomy 3:1-29	Luke 6:20-38	68:1-6	17:9-11
☐ 17	Deuteronomy 4:1-20	Luke 6:39-49	68:7-18	17:12-13
☐ 18	Deuteronomy 4:21-49	Luke 7:1-10	68:19-31	17:14-15
☐ 19	Deuteronomy 5:1-31	Luke 7:11-23	68:32-35	17:16
☐ 20	Deuteronomy 5:32-6:25	Luke 7:24-35	69:1-13	17:17-18
☐ 21	Deuteronomy 7:1-26	Luke 7:36-50	69:14-18	17:19-21
☐ 22	Deuteronomy 8:1-20	Luke 8:1-3	69:19-31	17:22
☐ 23	Deuteronomy 9:1-10:5	Luke 8:4-15	69:32-36	17:23
☐ 24	Deuteronomy 10:6-22	Luke 8:16-21	70:1-5	17:24-25
☐ 25	Deuteronomy 11:1-32	Luke 8:22-25	71:1-6	17:26
☐ 26	Deuteronomy 12:1-32	Luke 8:26-39	71:7-16	17:27-28
☐ 27	Deuteronomy 13:1-14:27	Luke 8:40-56	71:17-24	18:1
☐ 28	Deuteronomy 14:28-15:23	Luke 9:1-6	72:1-14	18:2-3
☐ 29	Deuteronomy 16:1-22	Luke 9:7-17	72:15-20	18:4-5
☐ 30	Deuteronomy 17:1-20	Luke 9:18-27	73:1-20	18:6-7

JULY

Day	OT	NT	Psalms	Proverbs
☐ 1	Deuteronomy 18:1-19:14	Luke 9:28-36	73:21-28	18:8
☐ 2	Deuteronomy 19:15-20:20	Luke 9:37-50	74:1-11	18:9-10
☐ 3	Deuteronomy 21:1-23	Luke 9:51-62	74:12-23	18:11-12
☐ 4	Deuteronomy 22:1-30	Luke 10:1-12	75:1-5	18:13
☐ 5	Deuteronomy 23:1-24:13	Luke 10:13-24	75:6-10	18:14-15
☐ 6	Deuteronomy 24:14-25:19	Luke 10:25-37	76:1-7	18:16-18
☐ 7	Deuteronomy 26:1-19	Luke 10:38-42	76:8-12	18:19
☐ 8	Deuteronomy 27:1-26	Luke 11:1-13	77:1-14	18:20-21
☐ 9	Deuteronomy 28:1-44	Luke 11:14-22	77:15-20	18:22
☐ 10	Deuteronomy 28:45-68	Luke 11:23-36	78:1-22	18:23-24
☐ 11	Deuteronomy 29:1-29	Luke 11:37-54	78:23-31	19:1-3
☐ 12	Deuteronomy 30:1-20	Luke 12:1-7	78:32-39	19:4-5
☐ 13	Deuteronomy 31:1-29	Luke 12:8-12	78:40-55	19:6-7
☐ 14	Deuteronomy 31:30-32:27	Luke 12:13-34	78:56-59	19:8-9
☐ 15	Deuteronomy 32:28-52	Luke 12:35-48	78:60-64	19:10-12
☐ 16	Deuteronomy 33:1-17	Luke 12:49-59	78:65-69	19:13-14
☐ 17	Deuteronomy 33:18-29	Luke 13:1-9	78:70-72	19:15-16
☐ 18	Deuteronomy 34:1-Joshua 1:18	Luke 13:10-21	79:1-8	19:17
☐ 19	Joshua 2:1-24	Luke 13:22-35	79:9-13	19:18-19
☐ 20	Joshua 3:1-17	Luke 14:1-6	80:1-13	19:20-21
☐ 21	Joshua 4:1-24	Luke 14:7-24	80:14-19	19:22-23
☐ 22	Joshua 5:1-15	Luke 14:25-35	81:1-7	19:24-25
☐ 23	Joshua 6:1-27	Luke 15:1-10	81:8-16	19:26
☐ 24	Joshua 7:1-26	Luke 15:11-32	82:1-5	19:27-29
☐ 25	Joshua 8:1-9:2	Luke 16:1-9	82:6-8	20:1
☐ 26	Joshua 9:3-10:11	Luke 16:10-18	83:1-8	20:2-3
☐ 27	Joshua 10:12-43	Luke 16:19-31	83:9-18	20:4-6
☐ 28	Joshua 11:1-23	Luke 17:1-10	84:1-4	20:7
☐ 29	Joshua 12:1-24	Luke 17:11-25	84:5-12	20:8-10
☐ 30	Joshua 13:1-33	Luke 17:26-37	85:1-7	20:11
☐ 31	Joshua 14:1-15	Luke 18:1-8	85:8-13	20:12

AUGUST

Day	OT	NT	Psalms	Proverbs
1	Joshua 15:1-12	Luke 18:9-17	86:1-7	20:13-15
2	Joshua 15:13-63	Luke 18:18-30	86:8-17	20:16-18
3	Joshua 16:1-17:18	Luke 18:31-43	87:1-3	20:19
4	Joshua 18:1-28	Luke 19:1-10	87:4-7	20:20-21
5	Joshua 19:1-31	Luke 19:11-27	88:1-12	20:22-23
6	Joshua 19:32-20:9	Luke 19:28-40	88:13-18	20:24-25
7	Joshua 21:1-42	Luke 19:41-48	89:1-6	20:26-27
8	Joshua 21:43-22:20	Luke 20:1-8	89:7-13	20:28-30
9	Joshua 22:21-34	Luke 20:9-26	89:14-18	21:1-2
10	Joshua 23:1-16	Luke 20:27-40	89:19-37	21:3
11	Joshua 24:1-28	Luke 20:41-47	89:38-45	21:4
12	Joshua 24:29-Judges 1:15	Luke 21:1-4	89:46-52	21:5-7
13	Judges 1:16-36	Luke 21:5-28	90:1-17	21:8-10
14	Judges 2:1-9	Luke 21:29-36	91:1-16	21:11-12
15	Judges 2:10-23	Luke 21:37-22:13	92:1-15	21:13
16	Judges 3:1-31	Luke 22:14-23	93:1-5	21:14-16
17	Judges 4:1-24	Luke 22:24-34	94:1-13	21:17-18
18	Judges 5:1-31	Luke 22:35-38	94:14-23	21:19-20
19	Judges 6:1-32	Luke 22:39-53	95:1-11	21:21-22
20	Judges 6:33-40	Luke 22:54-71	96:1-13	21:23-24
21	Judges 7:1-25	Luke 23:1-12	97:1-12	21:25-26
22	Judges 8:1-17	Luke 23:13-25	98:1-9	21:27
23	Judges 8:18-32	Luke 23:26-43	99:1-4	21:28-29
24	Judges 8:33-9:21	Luke 23:44-56	99:5-9	21:30-31
25	Judges 9:22-57	Luke 24:1-12	100:1-2	22:1
26	Judges 10:1-18	Luke 24:13-34	100:3-5	22:2-4
27	Judges 11:1-28	Luke 24:35-53	101:1-3	22:5-6
28	Judges 11:29-12:15	John 1:1-18	101:4-8	22:7
29	Judges 13:1-25	John 1:19-28	102:1-17	22:8-9
30	Judges 14:1-20	John 1:29-42	102:18-22	22:10-12
31	Judges 15:1-16:9	John 1:43-51	102:23-28	22:13

SEPTEMBER

Day	OT	NT	Psalms	Proverbs
1	Judges 16:10-31	John 2:1-11	103:1-12	22:14
2	Judges 17:1-18:21	John 2:12-25	103:13-22	22:15
3	Judges 18:22-31	John 3:1-15	104:1-7	22:16
4	Judges 19:1-30	John 3:16-21	104:8-23	22:17-19
5	Judges 20:1-48	John 3:22-30	104:24-30	22:20-21
6	Judges 21:1-25	John 3:31-4:3	104:31-35	22:22-23
7	Ruth 1:1-22	John 4:4-30	105:1-7	22:24-25
8	Ruth 2:1-3:6	John 4:31-42	105:8-15	22:26-27
9	Ruth 3:7-4:22	John 4:43-45	105:16-26	22:28-29
10	1 Samuel 1:1-23	John 4:46-54	105:27-36	23:1-3
11	1 Samuel 1:24-2:21	John 5:1-18	105:37-45	23:4-5
12	1 Samuel 2:22-3:18	John 5:19-23	106:1-2	23:6-8
13	1 Samuel 3:19-4:22	John 5:24-38	106:3-5	23:9-11
14	1 Samuel 5:1-6:12	John 5:39-47	106:6-12	23:12
15	1 Samuel 6:13-7:17	John 6:1-15	106:13-23	23:13-14
16	1 Samuel 8:1-22	John 6:16-21	106:24-31	23:15-16
17	1 Samuel 9:1-27	John 6:22-29	106:32-46	23:17-18
18	1 Samuel 10:1-27	John 6:30-42	106:47-48	23:19-21
19	1 Samuel 11:1-15	John 6:43-52	107:1-3	23:22
20	1 Samuel 12:1-25	John 6:53-71	107:4-32	23:23
21	1 Samuel 13:1-23	John 7:1-13	107:33-43	23:24
22	1 Samuel 14:1-23	John 7:14-30	108:1-4	23:25-28
23	1 Samuel 14:24-52	John 7:31-36	108:5-13	23:29-35
24	1 Samuel 15:1-35	John 7:37-53	109:1-21	24:1-2
25	1 Samuel 16:1-23	John 8:1-11	109:22-31	24:3-4
26	1 Samuel 17:1-40	John 8:12-20	110:1-3	24:5-6
27	1 Samuel 17:41-18:4	John 8:21-24	110:4-7	24:7
28	1 Samuel 18:5-30	John 8:25-30	111:1-4	24:8
29	1 Samuel 19:1-24	John 8:31-36	111:5-10	24:9-10
30	1 Samuel 20:1-34	John 8:37-59	112:1-3	24:11-12

OCTOBER

Day	OT	NT	Psalms	Proverbs
☐ 1	1 Samuel 20:35-21:15	John 9:1-13	112:4-10	24:13-14
☐ 2	1 Samuel 22:1-23	John 9:14-41	113:1-9	24:15-16
☐ 3	1 Samuel 23:1-29	John 10:1-10	114:1-8	24:17-20
☐ 4	1 Samuel 24:1-22	John 10:11-21	115:1-10	24:21-22
☐ 5	1 Samuel 25:1-44	John 10:22-29	115:11-18	24:23-25
☐ 6	1 Samuel 26:1-25	John 10:30-42	116:1-5	24:26
☐ 7	1 Samuel 27:1-28:25	John 11:1-29	116:6-14	24:27
☐ 8	1 Samuel 29:1-30:20	John 11:30-54	116:15-117:2	24:28-29
☐ 9	1 Samuel 30:21-31:13	John 11:55-12:8	118:1-7	24:30-34
☐ 10	2 Samuel 1:1-16	John 12:9-19	118:8-18	25:1-5
☐ 11	2 Samuel 1:17-2:11	John 12:20-36	118:19-26	25:6-8
☐ 12	2 Samuel 2:12-3:5	John 12:37-50	118:27-29	25:9-10
☐ 13	2 Samuel 3:6-39	John 13:1-20	119:1-8	25:11-14
☐ 14	2 Samuel 4:1-5:12	John 13:21-30	119:9-16	25:15
☐ 15	2 Samuel 5:13-6:23	John 13:31-38	119:17-24	25:16
☐ 16	2 Samuel 7:1-29	John 14:1-14	119:25-32	25:17
☐ 17	2 Samuel 8:1-18	John 14:15-26	119:33-40	25:18-19
☐ 18	2 Samuel 9:1-10:19	John 14:27-31	119:41-48	25:20-22
☐ 19	2 Samuel 11:1-27	John 15:1-17	119:49-58	25:23-24
☐ 20	2 Samuel 12:1-14	John 15:18-27	119:59-64	25:25-27
☐ 21	2 Samuel 12:15-31	John 16:1-16	119:65-72	25:28
☐ 22	2 Samuel 13:1-22	John 16:17-33	119:73-80	26:1-2
☐ 23	2 Samuel 13:23-39	John 17:1-26	119:81-88	26:3-5
☐ 24	2 Samuel 14:1-33	John 18:1-14	119:89-96	26:6-8
☐ 25	2 Samuel 15:1-22	John 18:15-24	119:97-104	26:9-12
☐ 26	2 Samuel 15:23-16:4	John 18:25-19:22	119:105-112	26:13-16
☐ 27	2 Samuel 16:5-23	John 19:23-30	119:113-120	26:17
☐ 28	2 Samuel 17:1-16	John 19:31-42	119:121-128	26:18-19
☐ 29	2 Samuel 17:17-29	John 20:1-18	119:129-136	26:20
☐ 30	2 Samuel 18:1-18	John 20:19-31	119:137-152	26:21-22
☐ 31	2 Samuel 18:19-19:10	John 21:1-14	119:153-159	26:23

NOVEMBER

YEAR ONE

Day	OT	NT	Psalms	Proverbs
☐ 1	2 Samuel 19:11-40	John 21:15-25	119:160-168	26:24-26
☐ 2	2 Samuel 19:41-20:13	Acts 1:1-14	119:169-176	26:27
☐ 3	2 Samuel 20:14-26	Acts 1:15-26	120:1-7	26:28
☐ 4	2 Samuel 21:1-22	Acts 2:1-21	121:1-4	27:1-2
☐ 5	2 Samuel 22:1-46	Acts 2:22-47	121:5-8	27:3
☐ 6	2 Samuel 22:47-23:23	Acts 3:1-11	122:1-5	27:4-6
☐ 7	2 Samuel 23:24-24:9	Acts 3:12-26	122:6-9	27:7-9
☐ 8	2 Samuel 24:10-25	Acts 4:1-22	123:1-2	27:10
☐ 9	1 Kings 1:1-37	Acts 4:23-37	123:3-4	27:11
☐ 10	1 Kings 1:38-53	Acts 5:1-11	124:1-6	27:12
☐ 11	1 Kings 2:1-25	Acts 5:12-42	124:7-8	27:13
☐ 12	1 Kings 2:26-3:2	Acts 6:1-6	125:1-3	27:14
☐ 13	1 Kings 3:3-28	Acts 6:7-15	125:4-5	27:15-16
☐ 14	1 Kings 4:1-34	Acts 7:1-10	126:1-3	27:17
☐ 15	1 Kings 5:1-6:13	Acts 7:11-29	126:4-6	27:18-20
☐ 16	1 Kings 6:14-38	Acts 7:30-43	127:1-2	27:21-22
☐ 17	1 Kings 7:1-26	Acts 7:44-50	127:3-5	27:23-27
☐ 18	1 Kings 7:27-51	Acts 7:51-60	128:1-4	28:1
☐ 19	1 Kings 8:1-21	Acts 8:1-13	128:5-6	28:2
☐ 20	1 Kings 8:22-66	Acts 8:14-24	129:1-4	28:3-5
☐ 21	1 Kings 9:1-28	Acts 8:25-40	129:5-8	28:6-7
☐ 22	1 Kings 10:1-29	Acts 9:1-9	130:1-5	28:8-10
☐ 23	1 Kings 11:1-28	Acts 9:10-25	130:6-8	28:11
☐ 24	1 Kings 11:29-12:19	Acts 9:26-35	131:1-132:9	28:12-13
☐ 25	1 Kings 12:20-13:6	Acts 9:36-43	132:10-12	28:14
☐ 26	1 Kings 13:7-34	Acts 10:1-8	132:13-18	28:15-16
☐ 27	1 Kings 14:1-31	Acts 10:9-23	133:1-2	28:17-18
☐ 28	1 Kings 15:1-24	Acts 10:24-33	133:3	28:19-20
☐ 29	1 Kings 15:25-16:28	Acts 10:34-48	134:1-135:4	28:21-22
☐ 30	1 Kings 16:29-17:24	Acts 11:1-18	135:5-12	28:23-24

DECEMBER

YEAR ONE

Day	OT	NT	Psalms	Proverbs
☐ 1	1 Kings 18:1-19	Acts 11:19-30	135:13-21	28:25-26
☐ 2	1 Kings 18:20-46	Acts 12:1-19	136:1-12	28:27-28
☐ 3	1 Kings 19:1-14	Acts 12:20-23	136:13-26	29:1
☐ 4	1 Kings 19:15-20:15	Acts 12:24-13:12	137:1-4	29:2-4
☐ 5	1 Kings 20:16-43	Acts 13:13-15	137:5-9	29:5-8
☐ 6	1 Kings 21:1-29	Acts 13:16-25	138:1-6	29:9-11
☐ 7	1 Kings 22:1-28	Acts 13:26-37	138:7-8	29:12-14
☐ 8	1 Kings 22:29-53	Acts 13:38-43	139:1-12	29:15-17
☐ 9	2 Kings 1:1-18	Acts 13:44-14:7	139:13-24	29:18
☐ 10	2 Kings 2:1-25	Acts 14:8-20	140:1-8	29:19-20
☐ 11	2 Kings 3:1-27	Acts 14:21-28	140:9-13	29:21-22
☐ 12	2 Kings 4:1-17	Acts 15:1-21	141:1-2	29:23
☐ 13	2 Kings 4:18-44	Acts 15:22-35	141:3-10	29:24-25
☐ 14	2 Kings 5:1-27	Acts 15:36-16:5	142:1-3	29:26-27
☐ 15	2 Kings 6:1-23	Acts 16:6-15	142:4-7	30:1-4
☐ 16	2 Kings 6:24-7:20	Acts 16:16-24	143:1-6	30:5-6
☐ 17	2 Kings 8:1-19	Acts 16:25-40	143:7-12	30:7-9
☐ 18	2 Kings 8:20-9:13	Acts 17:1-9	144:1-8	30:10
☐ 19	2 Kings 9:14-37	Acts 17:10-15	144:9-15	30:11-14
☐ 20	2 Kings 10:1-31	Acts 17:16-34	145:1-7	30:15-16
☐ 21	2 Kings 10:32-11:20	Acts 18:1-11	145:8-21	30:17
☐ 22	2 Kings 11:21-12:21	Acts 18:12-22	146:1-2	30:18-20
☐ 23	2 Kings 13:1-25	Acts 18:23-28	146:3-10	30:21-23
☐ 24	2 Kings 14:1-29	Acts 19:1-12	147:1-11	30:24-28
☐ 25	2 Kings 15:1-31	Acts 19:13-22	147:12-20	30:29-31
☐ 26	2 Kings 15:32-16:20	Acts 19:23-41	148:1-4	30:32
☐ 27	2 Kings 17:1-28	Acts 20:1-15	148:5-14	30:33
☐ 28	2 Kings 17:29-18:12	Acts 20:16-38	149:1	31:1-7
☐ 29	2 Kings 18:13-19:4	Acts 21:1-6	149:2-9	31:8-9
☐ 30	2 Kings 19:5-37	Acts 21:7-17	150:1-5	31:10-24
☐ 31	2 Kings 20:1-21	Acts 21:18-26	150:6	31:25-31

JANUARY

Day	OT	NT	Psalms	Proverbs
☐ 1	2 Kings 21:1-22:2	Acts 21:27-36	1:1-5	1:1-6
☐ 2	2 Kings 22:3-23:7	Acts 21:37-40	1:6	1:7-9
☐ 3	2 Kings 23:8-30	Acts 22:1-16	2:1-6	1:10-19
☐ 4	2 Kings 23:31-25:7	Acts 22:17-30	2:7-12	1:20-23
☐ 5	2 Kings 25:8-30	Acts 23:1-10	3:1-5	1:24-28
☐ 6	1 Chronicles 1:1-33	Acts 23:11-15	3:6-8	1:29-33
☐ 7	1 Chronicles 1:34-2:17	Acts 23:16-35	4:1-3	2:1-5
☐ 8	1 Chronicles 2:18-55	Acts 24:1-23	4:4-8	2:6-15
☐ 9	1 Chronicles 3:1-4:4	Acts 24:24-27	5:1-6	2:16-22
☐ 10	1 Chronicles 4:5-37	Acts 25:1-13	5:7-12	3:1-6
☐ 11	1 Chronicles 4:38-5:17	Acts 25:14-27	6:1-5	3:7-8
☐ 12	1 Chronicles 5:18-6:30	Acts 26:1-8	6:6-10	3:9-10
☐ 13	1 Chronicles 6:31-81	Acts 26:9-32	7:1-9	3:11-12
☐ 14	1 Chronicles 7:1-40	Acts 27:1-6	7:10-17	3:13-15
☐ 15	1 Chronicles 8:1-40	Acts 27:7-20	8:1	3:16-18
☐ 16	1 Chronicles 9:1-16	Acts 27:21-32	8:2-9	3:19-20
☐ 17	1 Chronicles 9:17-10:14	Acts 27:33-44	9:1-8	3:21-26
☐ 18	1 Chronicles 11:1-25	Acts 28:1-16	9:9-12	3:27-32
☐ 19	1 Chronicles 11:26-12:18	Acts 28:17-31	9:13-18	3:33-35
☐ 20	1 Chronicles 12:19-40	Romans 1:1-9	9:19-20	4:1-6
☐ 21	1 Chronicles 13:1-14:17	Romans 1:10-17	10:1-6	4:7-10
☐ 22	1 Chronicles 15:1-29	Romans 1:18-20	10:7-15	4:11-13
☐ 23	1 Chronicles 16:1-36	Romans 1:21-32	10:16	4:14-19
☐ 24	1 Chronicles 16:37-17:15	Romans 2:1-11	10:17-18	4:20-27
☐ 25	1 Chronicles 17:16-18:17	Romans 2:12-24	11:1-6	5:1-6
☐ 26	1 Chronicles 19:1-20:8	Romans 2:25-29	11:7	5:7-14
☐ 27	1 Chronicles 21:1-30	Romans 3:1-8	12:1-5	5:15-21
☐ 28	1 Chronicles 22:1-19	Romans 3:9-22	12:6-8	5:22-23
☐ 29	1 Chronicles 23:1-32	Romans 3:23-31	13:1-4	6:1-5
☐ 30	1 Chronicles 24:1-31	Romans 4:1-10	13:5-6	6:6-11
☐ 31	1 Chronicles 25:1-26:11	Romans 4:11-12	14:1-6	6:12-15

FEBRUARY

YEAR TWO

Day	OT	NT	Psalms	Proverbs
1	1 Chronicles 26:12-32	Romans 4:13-17	14:7	6:16-19
2	1 Chronicles 27:1-34	Romans 4:18-5:5	15:1-5	6:20-26
3	1 Chronicles 28:1-21	Romans 5:6-11	16:1-4	6:27-35
4	1 Chronicles 29:1-30	Romans 5:12-21	16:5-8	7:1-5
5	2 Chronicles 1:1-2:10	Romans 6:1-14	16:9-11	7:6-23
6	2 Chronicles 2:11-3:17	Romans 6:15-23	17:1-5	7:24-27
7	2 Chronicles 4:1-22	Romans 7:1-4	17:6-15	8:1-11
8	2 Chronicles 5:1-6:11	Romans 7:5-13	18:1-3	8:12-13
9	2 Chronicles 6:12-42	Romans 7:14-25	18:4-15	8:14-26
10	2 Chronicles 7:1-8:10	Romans 8:1-8	18:16-24	8:27-32
11	2 Chronicles 8:11-9:12	Romans 8:9-11	18:25-36	8:33-36
12	2 Chronicles 9:13-10:19	Romans 8:12-25	18:37-45	9:1-6
13	2 Chronicles 11:1-12:16	Romans 8:26-34	18:46-50	9:7-8
14	2 Chronicles 13:1-22	Romans 8:35-39	19:1-6	9:9-10
15	2 Chronicles 14:1-15:8	Romans 9:1-10	19:7-14	9:11-12
16	2 Chronicles 15:9-16:14	Romans 9:11-24	20:1-6	9:13-18
17	2 Chronicles 17:1-19	Romans 9:25-33	20:7-9	10:1-2
18	2 Chronicles 18:1-34	Romans 10:1-13	21:1-7	10:3-4
19	2 Chronicles 19:1-11	Romans 10:14-21	21:8-13	10:5
20	2 Chronicles 20:1-37	Romans 11:1-12	22:1-18	10:6-7
21	2 Chronicles 21:1-20	Romans 11:13-21	22:19-24	10:8-9
22	2 Chronicles 22:1-23:21	Romans 11:22-36	22:25-26	10:10
23	2 Chronicles 24:1-27	Romans 12:1-8	22:27-31	10:11-12
24	2 Chronicles 25:1-28	Romans 12:9-21	23:1-6	10:13-14
25	2 Chronicles 26:1-27:9	Romans 13:1-7	24:1-2	10:15-16
26	2 Chronicles 28:1-27	Romans 13:8-14	24:3-6	10:17
27	2 Chronicles 29:1-17	Romans 14:1-9	24:7-10	10:18
28*	2 Chronicles 29:18-36	Romans 14:10-15:4	25:1-7	10:19

Note: When Leap Year occurs, divide the February 28 reading between February 28 and February 29.

MARCH

YEAR TWO

Day	OT	NT	Psalms	Proverbs
1	2 Chronicles 30:1-20	Romans 15:5-13	25:8-15	10:20-21
2	2 Chronicles 30:21-31:21	Romans 15:14-22	25:16-22	10:22
3	2 Chronicles 32:1-23	Romans 15:23-33	26:1-8	10:23
4	2 Chronicles 32:24-33:13	Romans 16:1-9	26:9-12	10:24-25
5	2 Chronicles 33:14-34:13	Romans 16:10-20	27:1	10:26
6	2 Chronicles 34:14-33	Romans 16:21-27	27:2-3	10:27-28
7	2 Chronicles 35:1-27	1 Cor 1:1-9	27:4-6	10:29-30
8	2 Chronicles 36:1-23	1 Cor 1:10-17	27:7-10	10:31-32
9	Ezra 1:1-2:35	1 Cor 1:18-25	27:11-14	11:1-3
10	Ezra 2:36-70	1 Cor 1:26-2:5	28:1-5	11:4
11	Ezra 3:1-13	1 Cor 2:6-16	28:6-9	11:5-6
12	Ezra 4:1-24	1 Cor 3:1-4	29:1-2	11:7
13	Ezra 5:1-6:1	1 Cor 3:5-15	29:3-11	11:8
14	Ezra 6:2-22	1 Cor 3:16-23	30:1-3	11:9-11
15	Ezra 7:1-26	1 Cor 4:1-9	30:4-12	11:12-13
16	Ezra 7:27-8:20	1 Cor 4:10-21	31:1-2	11:14
17	Ezra 8:21-36	1 Cor 5:1-8	31:3-8	11:15
18	Ezra 9:1-15	1 Cor 5:9-13	31:9-18	11:16-17
19	Ezra 10:1-17	1 Cor 6:1-8	31:19-20	11:18-19
20	Ezra 10:18-44	1 Cor 6:9-20	31:21-22	11:20-21
21	Nehemiah 1:1-2:8	1 Cor 7:1-16	31:23-24	11:22
22	Nehemiah 2:9-3:14	1 Cor 7:17-24	32:1-7	11:23
23	Nehemiah 3:15-4:5	1 Cor 7:25-32	32:8-11	11:24-26
24	Nehemiah 4:6-5:13	1 Cor 7:33-40	33:1-5	11:27
25	Nehemiah 5:14-6:19	1 Cor 8:1-3	33:6-11	11:28
26	Nehemiah 7:1-60	1 Cor 8:4-13	33:12-19	11:29-31
27	Nehemiah 7:61-8:18	1 Cor 9:1-10	33:20-22	12:1
28	Nehemiah 9:1-21	1 Cor 9:11-18	34:1-3	12:2-3
29	Nehemiah 9:22-10:27	1 Cor 9:19-27	34:4-10	12:4
30	Nehemiah 10:28-39	1 Cor 10:1-13	34:11-14	12:5-7
31	Nehemiah 11:1-36	1 Cor 10:14-24	34:15-22	12:8-9

APRIL

YEAR TWO

Day	OT	NT	Psalms	Proverbs
☐ 1	Nehemiah 12:1-26	1 Cor 10:25-33	35:1-9	12:10
☐ 2	Nehemiah 12:27-13:14	1 Cor 11:1-12	35:10-18	12:11
☐ 3	Nehemiah 13:15-31	1 Cor 11:13-16	35:19-28	12:12-14
☐ 4	Esther 1:1-2:4	1 Cor 11:17-22	36:1-5	12:15-17
☐ 5	Esther 2:5-3:15	1 Cor 11:23-34	36:6-9	12:18
☐ 6	Esther 4:1-5:14	1 Cor 12:1-7	36:10-12	12:19-20
☐ 7	Esther 6:1-7:10	1 Cor 12:8-26	37:1-6	12:21-23
☐ 8	Esther 8:1-9:15	1 Cor 12:27-31	37:7-11	12:24
☐ 9	Esther 9:16-10:3	1 Cor 13:1-13	37:12-20	12:25
☐ 10	Job 1:1-22	1 Cor 14:1-9	37:21-29	12:26
☐ 11	Job 2:1-3:26	1 Cor 14:10-17	37:30-33	12:27-28
☐ 12	Job 4:1-5:27	1 Cor 14:18-25	37:34-40	13:1
☐ 13	Job 6:1-7:21	1 Cor 14:26-40	38:1-18	13:2-3
☐ 14	Job 8:1-9:24	1 Cor 15:1-11	38:19-22	13:4
☐ 15	Job 9:25-11:20	1 Cor 15:12-28	39:1-5	13:5-6
☐ 16	Job 12:1-13:28	1 Cor 15:29-44	39:6-13	13:7-8
☐ 17	Job 14:1-15:35	1 Cor 15:45-58	40:1-3	13:9-10
☐ 18	Job 16:1-18:4	1 Cor 16:1-9	40:4-10	13:11
☐ 19	Job 18:5-19:29	1 Cor 16:10-24	40:11-13	13:12-14
☐ 20	Job 20:1-21:21	2 Cor 1:1-7	40:14-17	13:15-16
☐ 21	Job 21:22-22:30	2 Cor 1:8-11	41:1-3	13:17-19
☐ 22	Job 23:1-24:25	2 Cor 1:12-22	41:4-13	13:20-23
☐ 23	Job 25:1-27:23	2 Cor 1:23-2:11	42:1-8	13:24-25
☐ 24	Job 28:1-29:17	2 Cor 2:12-14	42:9-11	14:1-2
☐ 25	Job 29:18-30:31	2 Cor 2:15-17	43:1-4	14:3-4
☐ 26	Job 31:1-32:1	2 Cor 3:1-11	43:5	14:5-6
☐ 27	Job 32:2-33:33	2 Cor 3:12-18	44:1-3	14:7-8
☐ 28	Job 34:1-37	2 Cor 4:1-4	44:4-7	14:9-10
☐ 29	Job 35:1-36:33	2 Cor 4:5-12	44:8-22	14:11-12
☐ 30	Job 37:1-24	2 Cor 4:13-18	44:23-26	14:13-14

MAY

Day	OT	NT	Psalms	Proverbs
1	Job 38:1-39:30	2 Cor 5:1-10	45:1-6	14:15-16
2	Job 40:1-41:34	2 Cor 5:11-14	45:7-17	14:17-19
3	Job 42:1-17	2 Cor 5:15-21	46:1-7	14:20-21
4	Ecclesiastes 1:1-2:23	2 Cor 6:1-2	46:8-11	14:22-24
5	Ecclesiastes 2:24-3:22	2 Cor 6:3-13	47:1-7	14:25
6	Ecclesiastes 4:1-5:9	2 Cor 6:14-7:1	47:8-9	14:26-27
7	Ecclesiastes 5:10-6:12	2 Cor 7:2-7	48:1-8	14:28-29
8	Ecclesiastes 7:1-8:8	2 Cor 7:8-10	48:9-14	14:30-31
9	Ecclesiastes 8:9-9:18	2 Cor 7:11-16	49:1-9	14:32-33
10	Ecclesiastes 10:1-11:10	2 Cor 8:1-9	49:10-20	14:34-35
11	Ecclesiastes 12:1-14	2 Cor 8:10-15	50:1-6	15:1-3
12	Song of Songs 1:1-2:17	2 Cor 8:16-20	50:7-23	15:4
13	Song of Songs 3:1-4:16	2 Cor 8:21-24	51:1-9	15:5-7
14	Song of Songs 5:1-6:13	2 Cor 9:1-8	51:10-19	15:8-10
15	Song of Songs 7:1-8:14	2 Cor 9:9-15	52:1-7	15:11
16	Isaiah 1:1-31	2 Cor 10:1-12	52:8-9	15:12-14
17	Isaiah 2:1-22	2 Cor 10:13-18	53:1-5	15:15-17
18	Isaiah 3:1-4:6	2 Cor 11:1-6	53:6	15:18-19
19	Isaiah 5:1-30	2 Cor 11:7-15	54:1-4	15:20-21
20	Isaiah 6:1-7:9	2 Cor 11:16-21	54:5-7	15:22-23
21	Isaiah 7:10-25	2 Cor 11:22-33	55:1-11	15:24-26
22	Isaiah 8:1-22	2 Cor 12:1-7	55:12-23	15:27-28
23	Isaiah 9:1-21	2 Cor 12:8-10	56:1-9	15:29-30
24	Isaiah 10:1-23	2 Cor 12:11-15	56:10-13	15:31-32
25	Isaiah 10:24-11:16	2 Cor 12:16-21	57:1-3	15:33
26	Isaiah 12:1-14:2	2 Cor 13:1-6	57:4-11	16:1-3
27	Isaiah 14:3-32	2 Cor 13:7-14	58:1-9	16:4-5
28	Isaiah 15:1-16:14	Galatians 1:1-10	58:10-11	16:6-7
29	Isaiah 17:1-18:7	Galatians 1:11-24	59:1-13	16:8-9
30	Isaiah 19:1-25	Galatians 2:1-10	59:14-17	16:10-11
31	Isaiah 20:1-21:17	Galatians 2:11-16	60:1-5	16:12-13

JUNE

YEAR TWO

Day	OT	NT	Psalms	Proverbs
1	Isaiah 22:1-25	Galatians 2:17-21	60:6-12	16:14-15
2	Isaiah 23:1-24:23	Galatians 3:1-9	61:1-3	16:16-17
3	Isaiah 25:1-26:21	Galatians 3:10-14	61:4-8	16:18
4	Isaiah 27:1-28:13	Galatians 3:15-22	62:1-8	16:19-20
5	Isaiah 28:14-29:14	Galatians 3:23-4:20	62:9-12	16:21-23
6	Isaiah 29:15-30:11	Galatians 4:21-31	63:1-5	16:24
7	Isaiah 30:12-31:9	Galatians 5:1-6	63:6-11	16:25
8	Isaiah 32:1-33:9	Galatians 5:7-12	64:1-9	16:26-27
9	Isaiah 33:10-35:10	Galatians 5:13-18	64:10	16:28-30
10	Isaiah 36:1-22	Galatians 5:19-26	65:1-4	16:31-33
11	Isaiah 37:1-29	Galatians 6:1-10	65:5-13	17:1
12	Isaiah 37:30-38:22	Galatians 6:11-18	66:1-7	17:2-3
13	Isaiah 39:1-40:17	Ephesians 1:1-14	66:8-20	17:4-5
14	Isaiah 40:18-41:16	Ephesians 1:15-23	67:1-3	17:6
15	Isaiah 41:17-42:9	Ephesians 2:1-10	67:4-7	17:7-8
16	Isaiah 42:10-43:13	Ephesians 2:11-22	68:1-6	17:9-11
17	Isaiah 43:14-44:8	Ephesians 3:1-11	68:7-18	17:12-13
18	Isaiah 44:9-45:10	Ephesians 3:12-21	68:19-31	17:14-15
19	Isaiah 45:11-46:13	Ephesians 4:1-8	68:32-35	17:16
20	Isaiah 47:1-48:11	Ephesians 4:9-16	69:1-13	17:17-18
21	Isaiah 48:12-49:12	Ephesians 4:17-24	69:14-18	17:19-21
22	Isaiah 49:13-50:11	Ephesians 4:25-32	69:19-31	17:22
23	Isaiah 51:1-23	Ephesians 5:1-9	69:32-36	17:23
24	Isaiah 52:1-53:12	Ephesians 5:10-33	70:1-5	17:24-25
25	Isaiah 54:1-55:13	Ephesians 6:1-9	71:1-6	17:26
26	Isaiah 56:1-57:14	Ephesians 6:10-24	71:7-16	17:27-28
27	Isaiah 57:15-58:14	Philippians 1:1-11	71:17-24	18:1
28	Isaiah 59:1-21	Philippians 1:12-26	72:1-14	18:2-3
29	Isaiah 60:1-22	Philippians 1:27-2:2	72:15-20	18:4-5
30	Isaiah 61:1-62:5	Philippians 2:3-18	73:1-20	18:6-7

JULY

YEAR TWO

Day	OT	NT	Psalms	Proverbs
☐ 1	Isaiah 62:6-64:12	Philippians 2:19-30	73:21-28	18:8
☐ 2	Isaiah 65:1-25	Philippians 3:1-3	74:1-11	18:9-10
☐ 3	Isaiah 66:1-9	Philippians 3:4-12	74:12-23	18:11-12
☐ 4	Isaiah 66:10-24	Philippians 3:13-21	75:1-5	18:13
☐ 5	Jeremiah 1:1-19	Philippians 4:1-7	75:6-10	18:14-15
☐ 6	Jeremiah 2:1-30	Philippians 4:8-23	76:1-7	18:16-18
☐ 7	Jeremiah 2:31-3:20	Colossians 1:1-10	76:8-12	18:19
☐ 8	Jeremiah 3:21-4:18	Colossians 1:11-17	77:1-14	18:20-21
☐ 9	Jeremiah 4:19-5:19	Colossians 1:18-27	77:15-20	18:22
☐ 10	Jeremiah 5:20-6:15	Colossians 1:28-2:7	78:1-22	18:23-24
☐ 11	Jeremiah 6:16-7:20	Colossians 2:8-12	78:23-31	19:1-3
☐ 12	Jeremiah 7:21-8:7	Colossians 2:13-23	78:32-39	19:4-5
☐ 13	Jeremiah 8:8-22	Colossians 3:1-11	78:40-55	19:6-7
☐ 14	Jeremiah 9:1-26	Colossians 3:12-17	78:56-59	19:8-9
☐ 15	Jeremiah 10:1-25	Colossians 3:18-4:6	78:60-64	19:10-12
☐ 16	Jeremiah 11:1-23	Colossians 4:7-18	78:65-69	19:13-14
☐ 17	Jeremiah 12:1-13:7	1 Thess 1:1-10	78:70-72	19:15-16
☐ 18	Jeremiah 13:8-14-10	1 Thess 2:1-8	79:1-8	19:17
☐ 19	Jeremiah 14:11-15:9	1 Thess 2:9-16	79:9-13	19:18-19
☐ 20	Jeremiah 15:10-16:15	1 Thess 2:17-3:13	80:1-13	19:20-21
☐ 21	Jeremiah 16:16-17:27	1 Thess 4:1-12	80:14-19	19:22-23
☐ 22	Jeremiah 18:1-23	1 Thess 4:13-5:3	81:1-7	19:24-25
☐ 23	Jeremiah 19:1-20:6	1 Thess 5:4-11	81:8-16	19-26
☐ 24	Jeremiah 20:7-21:14	1 Thess 5:12-28	82:1-5	19:27-29
☐ 25	Jeremiah 22:1-30	2 Thess 1:1-6	82:6-8	20:1
☐ 26	Jeremiah 23:1-20	2 Thess 1:7-12	83:1-8	20:2-3
☐ 27	Jeremiah 23:21-24:10	2 Thess 2:1-12	83:9-18	20:4-6
☐ 28	Jeremiah 25:1-38	2 Thess 2:13-17	84:1-4	20:7
☐ 29	Jeremiah 26:1-24	2 Thess 3:1-5	84:5-12	20:8-10
☐ 30	Jeremiah 27:1-22	2 Thess 3:6-18	85:1-7	20:11
☐ 31	Jeremiah 28:1-17	1 Timothy 1:1-11	85:8-13	20:12

AUGUST

Day	OT	NT	Psalms	Proverbs
☐ 1	Jeremiah 29:1-32	1 Timothy 1:12-20	86:1-7	20:13-15
☐ 2	Jeremiah 30:1-24	1 Timothy 2:1-7	86:8-17	20:16-18
☐ 3	Jeremiah 31:1-26	1 Timothy 2:8-15	87:1-3	20:19
☐ 4	Jeremiah 31:27-32:5	1 Timothy 3:1-5	87:4-7	20:20-21
☐ 5	Jeremiah 32:6-44	1 Timothy 3:6-16	88:1-12	20:22-23
☐ 6	Jeremiah 33:1-22	1 Timothy 4:1-6	88:13-18	20:24-25
☐ 7	Jeremiah 33:23-34:22	1 Timothy 4:7-16	89:1-6	20:26-27
☐ 8	Jeremiah 35:1-19	1 Timothy 5:1-16	89:7-13	20:28-30
☐ 9	Jeremiah 36:1-32	1 Timothy 5:17-25	89:14-18	21:1-2
☐ 10	Jeremiah 37:1-21	1 Timothy 6:1-11	89:19-37	21:3
☐ 11	Jeremiah 38:1-28	1 Timothy 6:12-21	89:38-46	21:4
☐ 12	Jeremiah 39:1-40:6	2 Timothy 1:1-8	89:47-52	21:5-7
☐ 13	Jeremiah 40:7-41:18	2 Timothy 1:9-18	90:1-17	21:8-10
☐ 14	Jeremiah 42:1-43:13	2 Timothy 2:1-7	91:1-16	21:11-12
☐ 15	Jeremiah 44:1-23	2 Timothy 2:8-21	92:1-15	21:13
☐ 16	Jeremiah 44:24-46:12	2 Timothy 2:22-26	93:1-5	21:14-16
☐ 17	Jeremiah 46:13-47:7	2 Timothy 3:1-17	94:1-13	21:17-18
☐ 18	Jeremiah 48:1-47	2 Timothy 4:1-5	94:14-23	21:19-20
☐ 19	Jeremiah 49:1-22	2 Timothy 4:6-22	95:1-11	21:21-22
☐ 20	Jeremiah 49:23-50:20	Titus 1:1-3	96:1-13	21:23-24
☐ 21	Jeremiah 50:21-46	Titus 1:4-16	97:1-12	21:25-26
☐ 22	Jeremiah 51:1-26	Titus 2:1-8	98:1-9	21:27
☐ 23	Jeremiah 51:27-53	Titus 2:9-15	99:1-4	21:28-29
☐ 24	Jeremiah 51:54-52:11	Titus 3:1-8	99:5-9	21:30-31
☐ 25	Jeremiah 52:12-34	Titus 3:9-15	100:1-2	22:1
☐ 26	Lamentations 1:1-22	Philemon 1:1-3	100:3-5	22:2-4
☐ 27	Lamentations 2:1-19	Philemon 1:4-25	101:1-3	22:5-6
☐ 28	Lamentations 2:20-3:24	Hebrews 1:1-8	101:4-8	22:7
☐ 29	Lamentations 3:25-66	Hebrews 1:9-14	102:1-17	22:8-9
☐ 30	Lamentations 4:1-22	Hebrews 2:1-13	102:18-22	22:10-12
☐ 31	Lamentations 5:1-22	Hebrews 2:14-18	102:23-28	22:13

SEPTEMBER

Day	OT	NT	Psalms	Proverbs
1	Ezekiel 1:1-28	Hebrews 3:1-12	103:1-12	22:14
2	Ezekiel 2:1-3:15	Hebrews 3:13-19	103:13-22	22:15
3	Ezekiel 3:16-4:17	Hebrews 4:1-11	104:1-7	22:16
4	Ezekiel 5:1-6:14	Hebrews 4:12-16	104:8-23	22:17-19
5	Ezekiel 7:1-27	Hebrews 5:1-11	104:24-30	22:20-21
6	Ezekiel 8:1-9:11	Hebrews 5:12-14	104:31-35	22:22-23
7	Ezekiel 10:1-22	Hebrews 6:1-10	105:1-7	22:24-25
8	Ezekiel 11:1-25	Hebrews 6:11-20	105:8-15	22:26-27
9	Ezekiel 12:1-28	Hebrews 7:1-10	105:16-26	22:28-29
10	Ezekiel 13:1-14:11	Hebrews 7:11-17	105:27-36	23:1-3
11	Ezekiel 14:12-15:8	Hebrews 7:18-25	105:37-45	23:4-5
12	Ezekiel 16:1-41	Hebrews 7:26-28	106:1-2	23:6-8
13	Ezekiel 16:42-63	Hebrews 8:1-6	106:3-5	23:9-11
14	Ezekiel 17:1-24	Hebrews 8:7-13	106:6-12	23:12
15	Ezekiel 18:1-32	Hebrews 9:1-5	106:13-23	23:13-14
16	Ezekiel 19:1-14	Hebrews 9:6-10	106:24-31	23:15-16
17	Ezekiel 20:1-26	Hebrews 9:11-23	106:32-46	23:17-18
18	Ezekiel 20:27-49	Hebrews 9:24-28	106:47-48	23:19-21
19	Ezekiel 21:1-32	Hebrews 10:1-7	107:1-3	23:22
20	Ezekiel 22:1-31	Hebrews 10:8-17	107:4-32	23:23
21	Ezekiel 23:1-27	Hebrews 10:18-23	107:33-43	23:24
22	Ezekiel 23:28-49	Hebrews 10:24-39	108:1-4	23:25-28
23	Ezekiel 24:1-25:11	Hebrews 11:1-7	108:5-13	23:29-35
24	Ezekiel 25:12-26:21	Hebrews 11:8-16	109:1-21	24:1-2
25	Ezekiel 27:1-36	Hebrews 11:17-23	109:22-31	24:3-4
26	Ezekiel 28:1-26	Hebrews 11:24-31	110:1-3	24:5-6
27	Ezekiel 29:1-21	Hebrews 11:32-40	110:4-7	24:7
28	Ezekiel 30:1-26	Hebrews 12:1-13	111:1-4	24:8
29	Ezekiel 31:1-18	Hebrews 12:14-24	111:5-10	24:9-10
30	Ezekiel 32:1-32	Hebrews 12:25-29	112:1-3	24:11-12

OCTOBER

YEAR TWO

Day	OT	NT	Psalms	Proverbs
☐ 1	Ezekiel 33:1-33	Hebrews 13:1-16	112:4-10	24:13-14
☐ 2	Ezekiel 34:1-31	Hebrews 13:17-25	113:1-9	24:15-16
☐ 3	Ezekiel 35:1-36:15	James 1:1-8	114:1-8	24:17-20
☐ 4	Ezekiel 36:16-38	James 1:9-18	115:1-10	24:21-22
☐ 5	Ezekiel 37:1-28	James 1:19-27	115:11-18	24:23-25
☐ 6	Ezekiel 38:1-23	James 2:1-17	116:1-5	24:26
☐ 7	Ezekiel 39:1-29	James 2:18-3:6	116:6-14	24:27
☐ 8	Ezekiel 40:1-27	James 3:7-18	116:15-117:2	24:28-29
☐ 9	Ezekiel 40:28-49	James 4:1-10	118:1-7	24:30-34
☐ 10	Ezekiel 41:1-26	James 4:11-17	118:8-18	25:1-5
☐ 11	Ezekiel 42:1-43:4	James 5:1-8	118:19-26	25:6-8
☐ 12	Ezekiel 43:5-27	James 5:9-20	118:27-29	25:9-10
☐ 13	Ezekiel 44:1-31	1 Peter 1:1-6	119:1-8	25:11-14
☐ 14	Ezekiel 45:1-12	1 Peter 1:7-12	119:9-16	25:15
☐ 15	Ezekiel 45:13-46:3	1 Peter 1:13-25	119:17-24	25:16
☐ 16	Ezekiel 46:4-24	1 Peter 2:1-10	119:25-32	25:17
☐ 17	Ezekiel 47:1-23	1 Peter.2:11-25	119:33-40	25:18-19
☐ 18	Ezekiel 48:1-35	1 Peter 3:1-7	119:41-48	25:20-22
☐ 19	Daniel 1:1-21	1 Peter 3:8-22	119:49-58	25:23-24
☐ 20	Daniel 2:1-23	1 Peter 4:1-6	119:59-64	25:25-27
☐ 21	Daniel 2:24-49	1 Peter 4:7-19	119:65-72	25:28
☐ 22	Daniel 3:1-30	1 Peter 5:1-14	119:73-80	26:1-2
☐ 23	Daniel 4:1-27	2 Peter 1:1-9	119:81-88	26:3-5
☐ 24	Daniel 4:28-37	2 Peter 1:10-21	119:89-96	26:6-8
☐ 25	Daniel 5:1-12	2 Peter 2:1-10	119:97-104	26:9-12
☐ 26	Daniel 5:13-31	2 Peter 2:11-22	119-105-112	26:13-16
☐ 27	Daniel 6:1-18	2 Peter 3:1-11	119:113-120	26:17
☐ 28	Daniel 6:19-28	2 Peter 3:12-18	119:121-128	26:18-19
☐ 29	Daniel 7:1-14	1 John 1:1-4	119:129-136	26:20
☐ 30	Daniel 7:15-28	1 John 1:5-10	119:137-152	26:21-22
☐ 31	Daniel 8:1-14	1 John 2:1-6	119:153-159	26:23

NOVEMBER

YEAR TWO

Day	OT	NT	Psalms	Proverbs
☐ 1	Daniel 8:15-27	1 John 2:7-17	119:160-168	26:24-26
☐ 2	Daniel 9:1-27	1 John 2:18-29	119:169-175	26:27
☐ 3	Daniel 10:1-11:1	1 John 3:1-6	120:1-7	26:28
☐ 4	Daniel 11:2-12	1 John 3:7-13	121:1-4	27:1-2
☐ 5	Daniel 11:13-35	1 John 3:14-24	121:5-8	27:3
☐ 6	Daniel 11:36-45	1 John 4:1-6	122:1-5	27:4-6
☐ 7	Daniel 12:1-13	1 John 4:7-21	122:6-9	27:7-9
☐ 8	Hosea 1:1-2:1	1 John 5:1-12	123:1-2	27:10
☐ 9	Hosea 2:2-3:5	1 John 5:13-21	123:3-4	27:11
☐ 10	Hosea 4:1-19	2 John 1:1-6	124:1-6	27:12
☐ 11	Hosea 5:1-15	2 John 1:7-13	124:7-8	27:13
☐ 12	Hosea 6:1-7:16	3 John 1:1-4	125:1-3	27:14
☐ 13	Hosea 8:1-9:17	3 John 1:5-15	125:4-5	27:15-16
☐ 14	Hosea 10:1-11:12	Jude 1:1-19	126:1-3	27:17
☐ 15	Hosea 12:1-14:9	Jude 1:20-25	126:4-6	27:18-20
☐ 16	Joel 1:1-2:32	Revelation 1:1-8	127:1-2	27:21-22
☐ 17	Joel 3:1-21	Revelation 1:9-20	127:3-5	27:23-27
☐ 18	Amos 1:1-15	Revelation 2:1-7	128:1-4	28:1
☐ 19	Amos 2:1-3:15	Revelation 2:8-17	128-5-6	28:2
☐ 20	Amos 4:1-5:9	Revelation 2:18-29	129:1-4	28:3-5
☐ 21	Amos 5:10-6:14	Revelation 3:1-6	129:5-8	28:6-7
☐ 22	Amos 7:1-8:3	Revelation 3:7-13	130:1-5	28:8-10
☐ 23	Amos 8:4-9:15	Revelation 3:14-22	130:6-8	28:11
☐ 24	Obadiah 1:1-14	Revelation 4:1-6	131:1-132:9	28:12-13
☐ 25	Obadiah 1:15-21	Revelation 4:7-11	132:10-12	28:14
☐ 26	Jonah 1:1-2:10	Revelation 5:1-8	132:13-18	28:15-16
☐ 27	Jonah 3:1-4:11	Revelation 5:9-14	133:1-2	28:17-18
☐ 28	Micah 1:1-2:13	Revelation 6:1-8	133:3	28:19-20
☐ 29	Micah 3:1-4:13	Revelation 6:9-17	134:1-135:4	28:21-22
☐ 30	Micah 5:1-6:8	Revelation 7:1-8	135:5-12	28:23-24

DECEMBER

YEAR TWO

Day	OT	NT	Psalms	Proverbs
1	Micah 6:9-7:20	Revelation 7:9-17	135:13-21	28:25-26
2	Nahum 1:1-2:13	Revelation 8:1-5	136:1-12	28:27-28
3	Nahum 3:1-19	Revelation 8:6-13	136:13-26	29:1
4	Habakkuk 1:1-2:11	Revelation 9:1-12	137:1-4	29:2-4
5	Habakkuk 2:12-3:19	Revelation 9:13-21	137:5-9	29:5-8
6	Zephaniah 1:1-2:15	Revelation 10:1-7	138:1-6	29:9-11
7	Zephaniah 3:1-20	Revelation 10:8-11	138:7-8	29:12-14
8	Haggai 1:1-15	Revelation 11:1-14	139:1-12	29:15-17
9	Haggai 2:1-23	Revelation 11:15-19	139:13-24	29:18
10	Zechariah 1:1-13	Revelation 12:1-9	140:1-8	29:19-20
11	Zechariah 1:14-21	Revelation 12:10-17	140:9-13	29:21-22
12	Zechariah 2:1-13	Revelation 12:18-13:10	141:1-2	29:23
13	Zechariah 3:1-10	Revelation 13:11-18	141:3-10	29:24-25
14	Zechariah 4:1-14	Revelation 14:1-12	142:1-3	29:26-27
15	Zechariah 5:1-11	Revelation 14:13-20	142:4-7	30:1-4
16	Zechariah 6:1-15	Revelation 15:1-4	143:1-6	30:5-6
17	Zechariah 7:1-14	Revelation 15:5-8	143:7-12	30:7-9
18	Zechariah 8:1-13	Revelation 16:1-11	144:1-8	30:10
19	Zechariah 8:14-23	Revelation 16:12-21	144:9-15	30:11-14
20	Zechariah 9:1-8	Revelation 17:1-8	145:1-7	30:15-16
21	Zechariah 9:9-17	Revelation 17:9-18	145:8-21	30:17
22	Zechariah 10:1-12	Revelation 18:1-10	146:1-2	30:18-20
23	Zechariah 11:1-17	Revelation 18:11-24	146:3-10	30:21-23
24	Zechariah 12:1-14	Revelation 19:1-10	147:1-11	30:24-28
25	Zechariah 13:1-9	Revelation 19:11-21	147:12-20	30:29-31
26	Zechariah 14:1-11	Revelation 20:1-10	148:1-4	30:32
27	Zechariah 14:12-21	Revelation 20:11-15	148:5-14	30:33
28	Malachi 1:1-14	Revelation 21:1-14	149:1	31:1-7
29	Malachi 2:1-17	Revelation 21:15-27	149:2-9	31:8-9
30	Malachi 3:1-18	Revelation 22:1-7	150:1-5	31:10-24
31	Malachi 4:1-6	Revelation 22:8-21	150:6	31:25-31

DAILY
JOURNAL
PAGES

DAILY LIFE JOURNAL

DAILY LIFE JOURNAL

DAILY LIFE JOURNAL

DAILY LIFE JOURNAL

DAILY LIFE JOURNAL

DAILY LIFE JOURNAL

DAILY LIFE JOURNAL

DAILY LIFE JOURNAL

DAILY LIFE JOURNAL

DAILY LIFE JOURNAL

DAILY LIFE JOURNAL

DAILY LIFE JOURNAL

DAILY LIFE JOURNAL

DAILY LIFE JOURNAL

DAILY LIFE JOURNAL

DAILY LIFE JOURNAL

Appendix

SCRIPTURES FOR COMMON PRAYER NEEDS

APPENDIX:

SCRIPTURES FOR
COMMON PRAYER NEEDS

As stated earlier, praying the Word and praying according to the Word are the soundest and surest ways to ensure that our praying is according to the will and ways of God. Praying in this manner gives our praying both divine accuracy and authority. It anchors our minds in truth and fills our hearts with peace and assurance that our praying will be acted on and answered.

In this section, common categories for praying have been laid out and listed to help point you to scriptures that speak to specific areas of need or focus. As you use these scriptures in your praying, meditate on them and memorize them as the Holy Spirit leads you.

FAMILY

- God sets the solitary in families; He brings out those who are bound into prosperity; But the rebellious dwell in a dry land. (Psalm 68:6)

- And he will turn the hearts of the fathers to the children, and the hearts of the children to their fathers, lest I come and strike the earth with a curse. (Malachi 4:6)

- Children, obey your parents in the Lord, for this is right. "Honor your father and mother," which is the first commandment with promise: "that it may be well with you and you may live long on the earth." (Ephesians 6:1-3)

- And you, fathers, do not provoke your children to wrath, but bring them up in the training and admonition of the Lord. (Ephesians 6:4)

- Children, obey your parents in all things, for this is well pleasing to the Lord. Fathers, do not provoke your children, lest they become discouraged. (Colossians 3:20-21)

FEAR

- When you lie down, you will not be afraid; Yes, you will lie down and your sleep will be sweet. (Proverbs 3:24)

- Keep me as the apple of Your eye; Hide me under the shadow of Your wings. (Psalm 17:8)

- For God has not given us a spirit of fear, but of power and of love and of a sound mind. (2 Timothy 1:7)

- Because you have made the LORD, who is my refuge,
  Even the Most High, your dwelling place, No evil shall befall you,
  Nor shall any plague come near your dwelling; (Psalm 91:9-10)

- For you did not receive the spirit of bondage again to fear, but you received the Spirit of adoption by whom we cry out, "Abba, Father." (Romans 8:15)

FRIENDSHIP

- I am a companion of all who fear You,
  And of those who keep Your precepts. (Psalm 119:63)

- A friend loves at all times, and a brother is born for adversity. (Proverbs 17:17)

- By this all will know that you are My disciples, if you have love for one another. (John 13:35)

- Can two walk together, unless they are agreed? (Amos 3:3)

- These things I command you, that you love one another. (John 15:17)

- As iron sharpens iron, so a man sharpens the countenance of his friend. (Proverbs 27:17)

- This is My commandment, that you love one another as I have loved you. Greater love has no one than this, than to lay down one's life for his friends. You are My friends if you do whatever I command you. (John 15:12-14)

- Though one may be overpowered by another, two can withstand him. And a threefold cord is not quickly broken. (Ecclesiastes 4:12)

HEALING

- But He was wounded for our transgressions, He *was* bruised for our iniquities; The chastisement for our peace *was* upon Him, and by His stripes we are healed. (Isaiah 53:5)

- He Himself bore our sins in His own body on the tree, that we, having died to sins, might live for righteousness—by whose stripes you were healed. (1 Peter 2:24)

- "And as you go, preach, saying, 'The kingdom of heaven is at hand.' Heal the sick, cleanse the lepers, raise the dead, cast out demons. Freely you have received, freely give." (Matthew 10:7-8)

- "And these signs will follow those who believe: In My name they will cast out demons; they will speak with new tongues; they will take up serpents; and if they drink anything deadly, it will by no means hurt them; they will lay hands on the sick, and they will recover." (Mark 16:17-18)

- If you diligently heed the voice of the Lord your God and do what is right in His sight, give ear to His commandments and keep all His statutes, I will put none of the diseases on you which I have brought on the Egyptians. For I *am* the Lord who heals you. (Exodus 15:26)

- ... how God anointed Jesus of Nazareth with the Holy Spirit and with power, who went about doing good and healing all who were oppressed by the devil, for God was with Him. (Acts 10:38)

LOVING OTHERS

- For this reason I bow my knees to the Father of our Lord Jesus Christ, from whom the whole family in heaven and earth is named, that He would grant you, according to the riches of His glory, to be strengthened with might through His Spirit in the inner man, that Christ may dwell in your hearts through faith; that you, being rooted and grounded in love, may be able to comprehend with all the saints what *is* the width and length and depth and height—to know the love of Christ which passes knowledge; that you may be filled with all the fullness of God. (Ephesians 3:14-19)

- Beloved, let us love one another, for love is of God; and everyone who loves is born of God and knows God. (1 John 4:7)

- My little children, let us not love in word or in tongue, but in deed and in truth. (1 John 3:18)

- But I say to you, love your enemies, bless those who curse you, do good to those who hate you, and pray for those who spitefully use you and persecute you, that you may be sons of your Father in heaven; for He makes His sun rise on the evil and on the good, and sends rain on the just and on the unjust. (Matthew 5:44-45)

- Finally, all of you be of one mind, having compassion for one another; love as brothers, be tenderhearted, be courteous; (1 Peter 3:8)

- By this all will know that you are My disciples, if you have love for one another. (John 13:35)

- Therefore, as the elect of God, holy and beloved, put on tender mercies, kindness, humility, meekness, longsuffering; bearing with one another, and forgiving one another, if anyone has a complaint against another; even as Christ forgave you, so you also must do. But above all these things put on love, which is the bond of perfection. (Colossians 3:12-14)

OBEDIENCE

- "He who has My commandments and keeps them, it is he who loves Me. And he who loves Me will be loved by My Father, and I will love him and manifest Myself to him." (John 14:21)

- Then Jesus answered and said to them, "Most assuredly, I say to you, the Son can do nothing of Himself, but what He sees the Father do; for whatever He does, the Son also does in like manner. (John 5:19)

- He who is not with Me is against Me, and he who does not gather with Me scatters. (Luke 11:23)

- "Therefore whoever hears these sayings of Mine, and does them, I will liken him to a wise man who built his house on the rock:" (Matthew 7:24)

PEACE

- You will keep him in perfect peace,
  Whose mind is stayed on You,
  Because he trusts in You.
  (Isaiah 26:3)

- Peace I leave with you, My peace I give to you; not as the world gives do I give to you. Let not your heart be troubled, neither let it be afraid. (John 14:27)

- Be anxious for nothing, but in everything by prayer and supplication, with thanksgiving, let your requests be made known to God; and the peace of God, which surpasses all understanding, will guard your hearts and minds through Christ Jesus. (Philippians 4:6-7)

- Blessed *are* the peacemakers, for they shall be called sons of God. (Matthew 5:9)

- Glory to God in the highest, and on earth peace, goodwill toward men! (Luke 2:14)

RELATIONSHIP WITH GOD

• And I will pray the Father, and He will give you another Helper, that He may abide with you forever— the Spirit of truth, whom the world cannot receive, because it neither sees Him nor knows Him; but you know Him, for He dwells with you and will be in you. (John 14:16-17)

• Jesus answered and said to him, "If anyone loves Me, he will keep My word; and My Father will love him, and We will come to him and make Our home with him." (John 14:23)

• Jesus said to him, "'You shall love the Lord your God with all your heart, with all your soul, and with all your mind.'" (Matthew 22:37)

• One thing I have desired of the Lord,
That will I seek:
That I may dwell in the house of the Lord
All the days of my life,
To behold the beauty of the Lord,
And to inquire in His temple.
(Psalm 27:4)

• For God so loved the world that He gave His only begotten Son, that whoever believes in Him should not perish but have everlasting life. (John 3:16)

• For I am persuaded that neither death nor life, nor angels nor principalities nor powers, nor things present nor things to come, nor height nor depth, nor any other created thing, shall be able to separate us from the love of God which is in Christ Jesus our Lord. (Romans 8:38-39)

SAFETY

- I will both lie down in peace, and sleep; For You alone, O Lord, make me dwell in safety. (Psalm 4:8)

- "For I will surely deliver you, and you shall not fall by the sword; but your life shall be as a prize to you, because you have put your trust in Me," says the Lord. (Jeremiah 39:18)

- The Lord also will be a refuge for the oppressed, a refuge in times of trouble. (Psalm 9:9)

- And have not shut me up into the hand of the enemy; You have set my feet in a wide place. (Psalm 31:8)

- The name of the Lord *is* a strong tower; The righteous run to it and are safe. (Proverbs 18:10)

- I do not pray that You should take them out of the world, but that You should keep them from the evil one. (John 17:5)

UNBELIEVERS

- Therefore I exhort first of all that supplications, prayers, intercessions, and giving of thanks be made for all men, for kings and all who are in authority, that we may lead a quiet and peaceable life in all godliness and reverence. For this is good and acceptable in the sight of God our Savior, who desires all men to be saved and to come to the knowledge of the truth. (1 Timothy 2:1-4)

- For it is the God who commanded light to shine out of darkness, who has shone in our hearts to *give* the light of the knowledge of the glory of God in the face of Jesus Christ.

- Let your light so shine before men, that they may see your good works and glorify your Father in heaven. (Matthew 5:16)

- And when He has come, He will convict the world of sin, and of righteousness, and of judgment: (John 16:8)

- For God so loved the world that He gave His only begotten Son, that whoever believes in Him should not perish but have everlasting life. (John 3:16)

- ... having your conduct honorable among the Gentiles, that when they speak against you as evildoers, they may, by your good works which they observe, glorify God in the day of visitation. (1 Peter 2:12)

- But even if our gospel is veiled, it is veiled to those who are perishing, whose minds the god of this age has blinded, who do not believe, lest the light of the gospel of the glory of Christ, who is the image of God, should shine on them. For we do not preach ourselves, but Christ Jesus the Lord, and ourselves your bondservants for Jesus' sake. For it is the God who commanded light to shine out of darkness, who has shone in our hearts to give the light of the knowledge of the glory of God in the face of Jesus Christ. (2 Corinthians 4:3-6)

UNITY

- Behold, how good and how pleasant *it is* for brethren to dwell together in unity! (Psalm 133:1)

- Live worthy of the calling you have received, with all lowliness and gentleness, with longsuffering, bearing with one another in love, endeavoring to keep the unity of the Spirit in the bond of peace. (Ephesians 4:1-3)

- Now the multitude of those who believed were of one heart and one soul; neither did anyone say that any of the things he possessed was his own, but they had all things in common. (Acts 4:32)

- Fulfill my joy by being like-minded, having the same love, being of one accord, of one mind. (Philippians 2:2)

- Now I plead with you, brethren, by the name of our Lord Jesus Christ, that you all speak the same thing, and that there be no divisions among you, but that you be perfectly joined together in the same mind and in the same judgment. (1 Corinthians 1:10)